To Stephenie Meyer, Andrew Niccol, Nick Wechsler, Will
Saoirse Ronan, and the entire cast and crew of *The Host*
And to Bob Wyatt, editor, author, auteur, friend, and mentor to many
— M.C.V.

Making a movie is a journey. The following filmmakers, representing
viewpoints from in front of and behind the camera, graciously shared their
perspectives on the creative journey of *The Host*:

THE PRODUCERS
NICK WECHSLER PRODUCER
STEVE SCHWARTZ PRODUCER
STEPHENIE MEYER AUTHOR AND PRODUCER
RAY ANGELIC EXECUTIVE PRODUCER
MEGHAN HIBBETT COPRODUCER

THE DIRECTOR
ANDREW NICCOL

ART DEPARTMENT
ANDY NICHOLSON PRODUCTION DESIGNER

CAMERA & LIGHT
ROBERTO SCHAEFER DIRECTOR OF PHOTOGRAPHY
PAUL OLINDE GAFFER
GEORGE "BUBBA" SHEFFIELD KEY GRIP

COSTUME, HAIR, & MAKEUP
ERIN BENACH COSTUME DESIGNER
CANDACE "CANDY" NEAL HAIR DEPARTMENT HEAD
VE NEILL MAKEUP DEPARTMENT HEAD
ROBERT SMITHSON CONTACT LENS TECHNICIAN

PROPS
GUILLAUME DELOUCHE PROP MASTER

EFFECTS
ELLEN SOMERS VISUAL EFFECTS SUPERVISOR/ PRODUCER
JACK LYNCH SPECIAL EFFECTS COORDINATOR

SCRIPT SUPERVISOR
SAM SULLIVAN

LOCATIONS
REBECCA PUCK STAIR LOCATION MANAGER, NEW MEXICO UNIT
WILLIS LEE LIAISON, NAVAJO NATION
FRED NORTH AERIAL COORDINATOR, NEW MEXICO UNIT

STUNTS
SAM HARGRAVE STUNT COORDINATOR
MELISSA STUBBS STUNT PERSON

THE ACTORS
SAOIRSE RONAN WANDA/MELANIE STRYDER
WILLIAM HURT JEB STRYDER
FRANCES FISHER MAGGIE STRYDER
DIANE KRUGER THE SEEKER
MAX IRONS JARED HOWE
JAKE ABEL IAN O'SHEA
LEE HARDEE AARON
MUSTAFA HARRIS BRANDT

If I stopped here and listened to the seductive suggestions of my host, I would truly be a traitor. **That was impossible. I was a soul.**

And yet I knew what I wanted, more powerfully and vividly than anything I had ever wanted in all the eight lives I'd lived. The image of Jared's face danced behind my eyelids when I blinked against the sun—not Melanie's memory this time, but my memory of hers. She forced nothing on me now. I could barely feel her in my head as she waited—I imagined her holding her breath, as if that were possible— for me to make my decision.

I could not separate myself from this body's wants.

It was me, more than I'd ever intended it to be. Did I want or did it want? Did that distinction even matter now?

—Wanderer, deciding to go into the desert in search of the beloved of Melanie Stryder, whose body she inhabits, *The Host*[1]

CONTENTS

The desert is dry as sun-bleached bone, its rocky terrain barren of green growth. Out of the stillness, coming over a ridge, walks a group of young men and a tall, older man carrying a shotgun. They lead a sunburned and blindfolded girl, while a white-haired woman brings up the rear, keeping a cautious distance from their captive. The grim procession silently moves down the rocky slopes of a soaring pinnacle of volcanic rock. They pass a motion-picture camera, equipment trucks, a scattering of onlookers—the parallel reality outside the moving images that audiences will eventually see on movie screens.

The camera stops, there's a call for "costume," and the white-haired woman heads for the welcome shade of an open tent. "This shoot has made my hair turn white!" actress Frances Fisher says, laughing, as

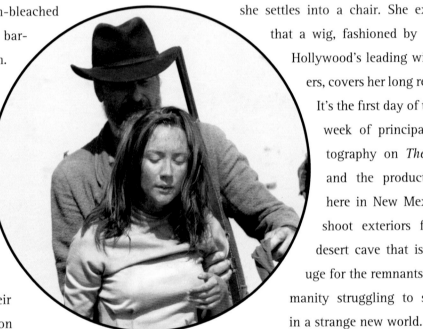

(Opposite page, clockwise from left) Aaron (Lee Hardee), Ian O'Shea (Jake Abel), Jeb Stryder (William Hurt), Maggie Stryder (Frances Fisher), Kyle O'Shea (Boyd Holbrook), and Brandt (Mustafa Harris) lead a captured Wanderer (Saoirse Ronan) through the desert.

she settles into a chair. She explains that a wig, fashioned by one of Hollywood's leading wigmakers, covers her long red hair. It's the first day of the last week of principal photography on *The Host*, and the production is here in New Mexico to shoot exteriors for the desert cave that is a refuge for the remnants of humanity struggling to survive in a strange new world.

"We've just found our niece, Melanie, in the desert," Fisher explains of the story point being filmed. "We've discovered she is inhabited by an alien named Wanderer, although we don't know Wanderer's name yet. William Hurt and I play brother and sister. I've been living in the cave for ten years; he's been living in the cave for I'll say twenty years. When the invasion comes, all the people who now live in the cave are truly the strongest to have crossed this desert by foot and survived. We're bringing her in, but I'm

Kyle and Maggie react violently when they realize the girl they've found is inhabited by an alien.

resistant. Jeb, Bill Hurt's character, has got a question about her. I don't! My character, Maggie, is against having an alien living among us. Maggie represents the people who have lost everything. We've already shot the opening scene where I first see her, and it's very emotional. I think my niece has come home, until I see that silver ring around her eyes! I see that she's now an alien—and I smack her. When they begin to bring her home I'm like, 'Why are you doing this? It's *dangerous*.'"

Someone calls out, "All right, first team!"

"It's too emotional, it's too much. All these peo-ple [living in the cave] have lost everybody. They're *dead*! The human race is dead. The bodies are walk-ing around, but they're inhabited by aliens. The rea-son I wanted to do this movie is that I wanted to see how that would be portrayed—the conversation in the head of Melanie, the two sides of it. We all have con-versations going on in our heads, our egos versus our higher consciousness and our conscience. I feel that's what's important in this movie, all the different grada-tions of that. I've gotta go—sorry."

Fisher moves off her chair and joins the other ac-tors as they head over the ridge for another take. As the shoot continues, Stephenie Meyer takes a seat on the shaded side of a production truck. The author of the novel on which the movie is based explains that this isn't the normal alien invasion scenario—for one thing, the aliens have won. "This story is not about the epic battle to save the earth. The war is over, that's done. And this story is told from the aliens' perspective."

The nervous cave dwellers don't realize it—although perhaps gun-toting Jeb has an inkling—but Melanie, the human host, and Wanderer, the "soul," as the aliens are known, may be the key to a new understanding between earthlings and the invaders from outer space. That is, if the scared, sunburned, and blindfolded girl survives.

The humans lead their captive into the caves where they make their home.

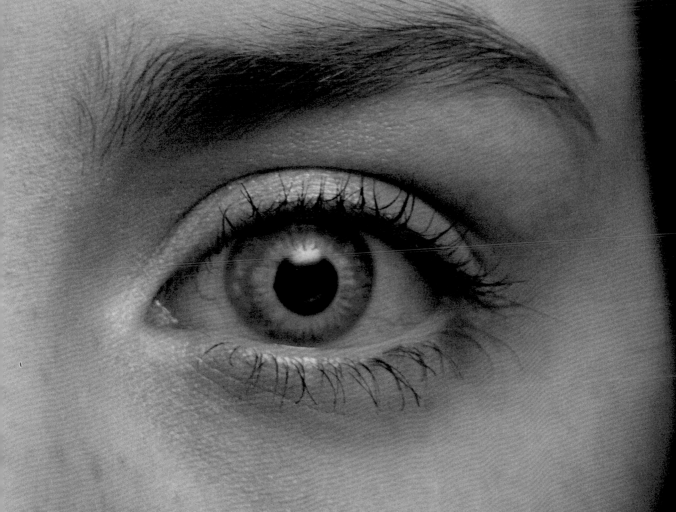

CHAPTER 1
POSSESSED

C an't you see—*everyone!* They're here already! *You're next!*"

The hysterical shouts are ignored by drivers on the freeway heading into Los Angeles as the screamer, a man dressed in a dirty, sweat-stained suit and tie, lurches between traffic lanes. Who would believe that this lunatic is a respected physician, much less his ramblings about what happened to his fellow citizens in the sleepy burg of nearby Santa Mira? "Their bodies were now hosts harboring an alien form of life, a cosmic form, which to survive must take over every human," the man realized before he escaped to warn the world.

Invasion of the Body Snatchers, the 1956 film starring Kevin McCarthy as the desperate doctor, was so unnerving to a preview audience that the head of Allied Artists, the low-rent studio releasing the picture, actually increased the budget to add new scenes, including the ending, in which a psychiatrist believes the doctor's story and goes to alert authorities, who presumably will ride like the cavalry to the rescue.[2]

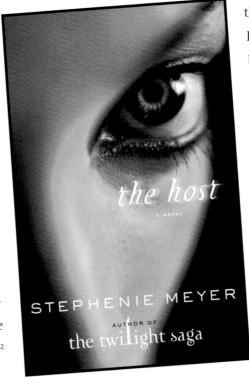

The alien invaders—pods fallen from outer space—absorb mind and memory, even cellular and genetic makeup, but empty their hosts of troublesome emotions like love and compassion. As with any story of possession, whether by demons or by the dark side that can overwhelm conscience and personality (Dr. Jekyll, meet Mr. Hyde), *Invasion* spoke to fears of loss of control and the extinction of self.

Alien possession is the theme of Stephenie Meyer's novel *The Host*, published by Little, Brown in 2008. That year saw the release of a movie adaptation of Meyer's debut novel, *Twilight*, the first in what has become a billion-dollar film franchise. The four bestselling Twilight Saga novels chart the course of teenager Bella Swan's romance with Edward Cullen, a high school classmate who happens to be a vampire. In the story, Meyer deftly turns vampire myth on its head. Her vampires, for example, don't flee to their coffins at dawn to slumber until dusk, safe from the sunshine that extinguishes them; her vampires don't sleep, and sunshine only makes their skin

Stephenie Meyer's Twilight Saga (right) has sold millions of copies around the world and been the basis for a billion-dollar film franchise. *The Host* (above), also a bestseller, is her first novel for adults.

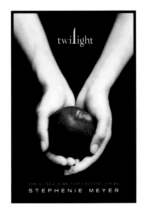

sparkle. Similarly, her vision of alien possession is not an emotion-destroying colonization of a host body. As Meyer asks in *The Host*, what if an alien took possession, the host's consciousness survived, and both minds amicably coexisted? What if intruder and host came to share memories, hopes, and dreams? What if they become a bridge between their tribes?

"It's much more fun to create your own mythology than to work within the limitations of one that already exists," Meyer said. "Sometimes people get upset with you—'Real vampires, don't [do this or that],' which is obviously funny on many levels. With aliens you have a lot more freedom because there aren't set rules: 'This must be the way of aliens.' It was fun to come up with my own species of creatures and all their worlds."

The inspiration for *Twilight* came to Meyer as a dream of a forest meadow where a young girl has an intense conversation with an incredibly handsome male vampire. *The Host* took possession of Meyer's imagination during a waking dream, one with origins in her childhood love of storytelling. "*The Host* is the root of who I am as a writer, I think," Meyer mused.

Meyer, who grew up in Phoenix, recalls childhood "vacations"—she adds the ironic quotation marks—during which her parents' idea of a getaway for their six children was to drive to a relative's home for a sojourn, which often ended abruptly with a long drive back in the middle of the night. "This was before TV and electronics in cars, so you're basically staring out the window or beating up your little brother. To keep sane on these long trips I would tell myself stories. We would drive through the desert to where we were going, and a lot of the stories were set in that scenery."

Flash forward to another car trip through the Arizona desert, this time with Meyer at the wheel and

"I like to write about things I wouldn't get to live, and *The Host* is the furthest out I've gone so far. I got to be an alien new to this planet and try to look at things with fresh eyes. What would be beautiful, what would be different, what would stick out if you were really brand-new here?"

—**Stephenie Meyer**, author and producer

kids of her own in the backseat. They were quietly watching a movie and Meyer found herself returning to her childhood game of making up stories. "I was bored and sort of coasting mentally and starting the story when I found myself halfway into the idea: what if you had two distinct personalities in one body and they both loved the same person? Something must have triggered it, but I don't know what it was. I just found myself in the middle of imagining this little conflict when I realized, 'Hey, this is an idea I could play with—this could be a full story.' We were

probably around Page, [Arizona], so that became the natural setting. It was a desert story from then on."

In *The Host*, beings from outer space known as souls seek to perfect life on other worlds—but first they inhabit the bodies of a planet's major life form. Earth falls, but many humans prefer suicide to possession, including young Melanie Stryder, who leaps down an elevator shaft. Her broken body is retrieved by the invaders, healed by their miraculous medicine, and supplied with a soul, one with the chosen name of Wanderer, or Wanda, as she comes to be known.

Melanie's consciousness survives, and she begins to share with Wanda her thoughts and memories, especially of her lost love, Jared, and her younger brother, Jamie. This is of concern to Wanderer's Seeker, one of the enforcers of soul society, who warns her that fewer than 20 percent of souls survive when a human host consciousness lives on and takes over.[3] But Wanda and Melanie bond and escape into the Arizona desert, guided by Melanie's memories of Stryder Ranch, the family spread near Picacho Peak. They hope to find Jared, Jamie, Uncle Jeb, and any of the Stryder clan who are still human.

Veteran film producer Nick Wechsler, whose Nick Wechsler Productions include *The Road* (2009), an adaptation of Cormac McCarthy's novel about a father and son wandering in a postapocalyptic America, was into his second reading of *The Host* when he decided to contact Meyer about acquiring film rights. By then *The Host* was already a bestseller. "In a way, I was late to the game and very surprised the rights were still available," Wechsler noted. "But the conceit

The desert setting plays an important part in both *The Host* novel and the film.

Saoirse Ronan plays the dual role of Melanie Stryder, a human, and Wanderer, a soul.

A standoff between souls and human rebels (top). Jared Howe (Max Irons) and Ian face off as Wanderer, known as Wanda, looks on (bottom).

of two consciousnesses in one body was a challenging idea to other potential financiers and distributors. I also found that Stephenie was up to her eyeballs doing the Twilight movies, and in no big rush to convert *The Host* into a film." That combination of factors, Wechsler concluded, allowed him the opening to secure the rights.

Wechsler brought aboard two producing partners he'd worked with on *The Road*, the husband-and-wife team of Steve and Paula Mae Schwartz of Chockstone Pictures. "The three of us are sci-fi buffs, and we were all interested in doing a project about first contact [with extraterrestrials]," Steve Schwartz recalled. "*The Host* had a unique take on first contact, with the hopefulness provided by the possibility of interspecies love. We thought it had elements that would appeal to Stephenie's core audience but also cross over to men, with its theme of resistance and survival. And while the book was definitely a fantasy/romance, it also had some interesting ideas for an audience to chew on."

With Meyer joining as a producer, the nucleus of the production was formed. The challenges ahead were enormous—securing a studio and distributor, arranging financing, hiring cast and crew, finding soundstages and filming locations. But it all began with the script. As with any adaptation of a book to the movie medium, hard choices had to be made. "I knew that figuring out how to turn a six-hundred-page novel that's epic in scope into a two-hour movie would be challenging," Wechsler noted. "You always have to have a clear plan in your head."

The answer to that seminal challenge lay in the choice of director, and the direction for that choice

Producer Nick Wechsler

"We thought it had elements that would appeal to Stephenie's core audience but also cross over to men, with its theme of resistance and survival."

emerged when Wechsler asked Meyer to name her top ten science-fiction movies. "I wanted to gauge her sensibilities so that I could cast the right filmmaker."

Meyer's top-ten list included *The Truman Show* (1998), about a man, Truman Burbank, who unknowingly lives in a controlled environment where he's the subject of the ultimate reality TV show, and *Gattaca* (1997), set in a near future of genetically perfected "Valids" and natural-birth "Invalids," in which a natural-born dreamer attempts to subvert the system to realize his vision of flying space missions. What these movies had in common was Andrew Niccol, a filmmaker from New Zealand who wrote the screenplay for *The Truman Show* and wrote and directed *Gattaca*. Wechsler and Niccol were friends, and Wechsler's production partners agreed to send Niccol the novel. "He loved it—he thought it was in his groove," Wechsler recalled.

Niccol had demonstrated a special talent for making visionary movies on a budget. *Gattaca*, for example, did not rely on elaborate effects and sets but used locations, lighting, and art direction to create the illusion of its future world. That resourcefulness was key to *The Host*, a production that would not have major studio backing but would take an "indie" approach. "Andrew's films have all been modestly budgeted by Hollywood standards," Wechsler said. "So it was not only his eye and taste but his ability to figure out how to pull off his amazing vision in a practical, not overly expensive way that made him interesting to the producers."

Wechsler also felt that Niccol, as a writer, understood the dynamics of adaptation—it was a potential deal-breaker if author and director had conflicting visions. Meyer worked with Niccol on the script but gave him full credit as screenwriter. "Making a book into a movie is a lot of give-and-take, but an author goes in knowing things have to change," explained Meghan Hibbett, Meyer's partner in Fickle Fish Films (a production company dedicated to literary adaptations) and a coproducer and intermediary between director and author when Meyer wasn't on set. "*The Host* is a lot to condense into script form. I couldn't do it, and Stephenie has said there's no way she could do it. People with specific screenwriting talent, like [screenwriter] Melissa Rosenberg, who adapted the Twilight books, and Andrew on this one, have the ability to condense everything into a movie that makes sense and has the dramatic beats and emotional levels you get reading the book."

"The story grabbed me right away," Andrew Niccol said. "We often talk about having inner conflicts, but in this story it's literally true. The fact that the alien race is better for the world than we are also drew me to the project. Alien beings are mostly depicted as the enemy, but what if the aliens are more humane than humans? I thought it was interesting to explore that

Souls use sprays rather than weapons to subdue their adversaries.

"Andrew got into the world and came up with things I liked better than what I did in the novel. For example, the Seekers don't use guns at all. In the novel it's sort of a necessary evil, where they're dealing with these fighting humans. I like this way better, because they've come up with other ways. They use sprays."

—Stephenie Meyer

Director Andrew Niccol on set

idea. In fact, with Stephenie's blessing, I took the idea further. In the novel, the Seekers carry guns, which we replaced with a futuristic Mace called Peace."

Executive producer Ray Angelic was a key member of the producing team and would ride herd on the budget and production schedule for the projected 2013 release. He made his first pass early in 2011, from breaking down the script to crunching budget numbers and contemplating locations. As the producers shopped the movie around, there were spikes in interest, cooling-down periods, even the consideration of other directors—all par for the course, Angelic noted. "I find that no matter how viable and interesting they sound, or even as much of a following [as] a project may have, few come together very quickly. This was the normal gestation period."

To distribute the film in foreign and domestic

"The story grabbed me right away."

markets, the production team chose Open Road Films, a theatrical distribution company formed in 2011 as a joint venture between AMC Theatres and Regal Cinemas. The company's CEO was Tom Ortenberg, who spent twelve years as president of theatrical films at Lionsgate Entertainment, a successful independent studio whose releases range from the award-winning *Monster's Ball* and *Crash* to the commercially popular *Saw* horror franchise. "I had done some business with Tom Ortenberg in the past and had a really good relationship with him," Wechsler explained. "It was the whole combination of a new company and a joint venture between two of the biggest theater companies in the United States—the idea of somebody kind of scrappy and needing to succeed, who looked at *The Host* as a big asset and potential franchise. That was the first choice for each of us, an easy path to go down."

The independent financing came together through Inferno Entertainment. Wechsler puts the budget in the mid-$40 million range—"a fairly handsome amount for an independent film," he notes—but the actual production budget was smaller. "On an independently financed film you have millions of dollars in bond fees, financing fees, legal fees, and you have to build in a ten percent contingency that you don't really get to use unless there's an emergency," Angelic explained. "So a big chunk of the budget is money you don't get to use to make the movie."

Budget concerns, as with any movie, dictated many creative choices. As in the novel, the screenplay included Wanda's memories of her host bodies on other worlds, sequences that would have to be created using three-dimensional computer graphics (CG) animation. Angelic had always red-flagged the planetary flashbacks, and when bids from visual effects houses arrived with price tags in the millions, the sequences became among the first items in the script to be cut.

Nick Wechsler explains that he had the money that might have been used to show Wanda's other worlds, but there were also creative concerns. "We all thought, 'Wouldn't it be great to have some of the events on other planets pepper our film?' Then we started thinking about what an intimate and emotionally intense journey it was for our character on our planet. We came to the conclusion that every time we'd do a three-minute drama on another planet, it would emotionally take the audience out of the flow of action for our character on Earth.

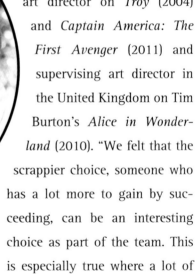

Director of photography Roberto Schaefer

Other people, as we were pulling together the money, also questioned whether we needed the flashbacks, if that was the best way to allocate our resources. Sometimes you get smarter about stuff as you get deeper into the process."

As budget, financing, and scheduling came together, so did the hiring of production department heads. "With most films you want your director to come up with ideas for the people he's interested in working with," Wechsler explained. "It's our job as producers to say, 'Hey, that's a good idea,' or maybe have questions about that choice. Andrew is very sure of his artistry and what it demands in terms of complementary partners."

Two key hires, on this or any movie, were production designer and director of photography (DP). The decision to hire Andy Nicholson as production designer was "a little bit of a wild card," according to Wechsler. Nicholson had largely worked in the art department under production designers, including being art director on *Troy* (2004) and *Captain America: The First Avenger* (2011) and supervising art director in the United Kingdom on Tim Burton's *Alice in Wonderland* (2010). "We felt that the scrappier choice, someone who has a lot more to gain by succeeding, can be an interesting choice as part of the team. This is especially true where a lot of more established production designers might have said, 'What you want to do is overwhelming, and you don't have enough money in your budget to do it.' This as opposed to someone who thinks, 'I'm going

Midcentury modern architecture helps depict the futuristic world of the souls.

to figure this out, no matter what.'" (Art director Beat Frutiger would lead *The Host*'s art department under Nicholson.)

DP Roberto Schaefer, whose feature credits range from *Monster's Ball* (2001) to *Finding Neverland* (2004) and the James Bond action epic *Quantum of Solace* (2008), was recommended to the production. "I got very excited, because I'm a big fan of Andrew's movies, especially *Gattaca*, which for me is a visual masterpiece," Schaefer recalled. "I love midcentury modern, I kind of grew up in it, and that was the visual style for the future world of *Gattaca*. The story takes place in the future, but it was the architecture and automobiles of the sixties. The movie had a strong architectural look, with compositional framing. He used the Citroën DS convertible, the Studebaker Avanti, and a few other cars like that, but he put in sounds like they were electric or hydrogen-powered."

Meanwhile, the hunt was on for filming locations. The cave, a major setting, had to be realized both on a soundstage for the interior space and in real desert for exteriors. For the latter, New Mexico, which had tax incentives, was an easy call over Arizona, where much of the novel is set. But Andrew Niccol's favorite architectural style—midcentury modern, with its clean and unadorned structures and natural, unified design—was absent in Albuquerque, as were locations needed to portray preinvasion times and the perfect world the aliens create after their invasion. But Louisiana had soundstages, locations, a filmmaking infrastructure, and alluring tax incentives. *The Host* would be a two-state production.

An initial location scout was made through the film commissions of New Mexico and Louisiana. In July 2011, Ray Angelic followed up with a solo scout to Louisiana's major filmmaking centers: New Orleans, Baton Rouge, and Shreveport. For New Mexico, Angelic felt everything they needed would be in and around Albuquerque. He had sent the film commission the requisite script pages and descriptions of ideal

Horseshoe Mesa and Shiprock (top two) were used to show exteriors of the caves in which the renegade humans live. The Aperture Center in Albuquerque and the First National Bank of Commerce in New Orleans (bottom two) served as locations in the souls' world.

locations, but in this instance he didn't place distance restrictions, figuring that potential locations would be an easy drive from Albuquerque. But the commission's report included tantalizing photos of Shiprock, a spire of volcanic rock rising from the desert, with a "tail," or spinelike wall of rock, running from its slopes—and Shiprock is a four-hour drive from Albuquerque, tucked up in the northwestern Four Corners region, on old Route 666, once known as Devil's Highway. "Of course, Shiprock is the most dramatic landscape," Angelic said. "Andrew saw the photos and immediately fell in love with it, and there was no way we weren't going to Shiprock. This was much to my chagrin in prep, when I was saying we couldn't go to yet another distant overnight location. At the end of the day, he wanted it badly enough, and was resourceful and responsible enough, that we all came up with a game plan that allowed us to shoot there, within our budget and schedule."

Shiprock was in the first visual presentation the director e-mailed to Andy Nicholson. The fall of 2011 "started it off" for Nicholson, including a whirlwind location scout that October. Roberto Schaefer hadn't yet come onto the production, so Niccol, Nicholson, and Angelic flew to Louisiana to visit the three film centers to look at potential stage space and locations. From there they flew to New Mexico and visited Albuquerque and Farmington, the biggest town near Shiprock. Some thirty miles away, on Navajo land (like Shiprock), they scouted a grouping of four mesas whose configuration led them to dub the location "Horseshoe Mesa." "It was a massive scout," Nicholson recalled. "But coming to New Mexico for the open

Jared meets Melanie on a raid while looking for food (top). Jared and Melanie in a flashback sequence (bottom).

spaces and desert stuff was just mind-blowing. In Shiprock alone, where the light changes all the time, we took about four thousand photographs."

Rebecca Puck Stair, the New Mexico–based location manager who would have to secure agreements for the desired locations, noted that the director did not want the usual striped and wind-shaped rock formations. "Andrew called them 'cartoonish.' He didn't want hoodoos, winding canyons, and the dramatic scenery a lot of other moviemakers respond to and are interested in. He really liked this bleak, dry landscape

with no vegetation that stretches out to nowhere. That's why we ended up in Farmington, because this place offers a scale you just can't find anywhere else in the state. You can see Shiprock sixty miles away, this huge formation rising out of the flat landscape."

Roberto Schaefer was soon on board and a participant in all subsequent location scouting. "It's funny—our first two or three scouts in New Mexico, it was under snow," Angelic recalled. "It's hard to get a director and a director of photography to sign off on what is supposed to be a hot, arid desert location

when it's cold and covered with snow. But at the end of the day they did."

Schaefer knew Niccol had shot his previous film, *In Time* (a 2011 release about a dystopian, genetically engineered future), using the Arri Alexa digital camera. The DP had shot commercials with the Alexa, never a feature, but was happy with the director's desire to use the camera for *The Host*. "When I go into a film, I don't want to approach it too much like I have these strong ideas, if the director has something different in mind," he said. "If I feel strongly enough, I'll propose what I have in mind, and see how they react. But Andrew and I have a similar aesthetic; we were pretty much on the same page. I also had a great working relationship with Andy Nicholson, who was very collaborative and totally open to my needs and requests and thoughts. We all worked as a team. It was tough, because the story had big underground caves and smaller caves, and you're trying to figure out what makes sense. How do you have an underground set that has light all the time? How do you handle day scenes and night scenes? Have they put in visible electric fixtures? Is it some sort of science we don't know about because it's somewhat in the future? How does it all work and where is the logic and where do you suspend disbelief and go with what works and just try to make it look right?"

By then the production had its soundstage in Louisiana. The labyrinthine "hero" cave of the human survivors would be built on a stage at Celtic Media Centre in Baton Rouge. At Albuquerque they'd shoot a high-speed sequence of Seekers chasing humans, while sand dunes outside the city would be where Wanda/Mel first searches for Uncle Jeb's cabin. "I'd say about eighty to ninety percent of the location issues had been worked out before Christmas of 2011," Angelic estimated. "But we still came in the first week or two

William Hurt and Frances Fisher as brother and sister Jeb and Maggie Stryder

of January to work out the Farmington, New Mexico, thing. That was the last challenge, locationwise. Shiprock was going to be this iconic landmark in the desert that Wanda/Mel wanders toward and that we see in flashbacks. The bulk of the [cave exterior] work was going to be in and around what the locals call Flat Top, and what we called Horseshoe Mesa."

The rest of the production team was assembled, including three-time Oscar winner Ve Neill leading the makeup department and Candace "Candy" Neal the hair department, Erin Benach as costume designer, Jack Lynch coordinating the special effects team, Ellen Somers as visual effects supervisor and producer, and veteran prop master Guillaume Delouche in charge of the props department.

The cast had such acclaimed and veteran performers as Frances Fisher, whose films include *Unforgiven* (1992), and Oscar-winner William Hurt. Diane

> "I don't want to say I was panicked, but I knew we needed to cast the perfect person to play the lead."

Kruger, who played Helen in *Troy* and an undercover agent in *Inglourious Basterds* (2009), would star as the main Seeker obsessed with capturing Wanda. The cast also featured a healthy crop of new young actors.

But the most important casting decision was an actress who could embody both the alien Wanderer and the human host Melanie Stryder. "I don't want to say I was panicked, but I knew we needed to cast the perfect person to play the lead," Nick Wechsler recalled. "We knew the movie would rest, or die, upon that choice."

During the search for their lead actress, Wechsler went to a movie that happened to star an actress who at one point had been considered for the role of Wanderer/Melanie. "About ten minutes into that movie, the hairs on the back of my neck were kind of standing up, and I thought, '*This is the girl*. This has to be the one!'"

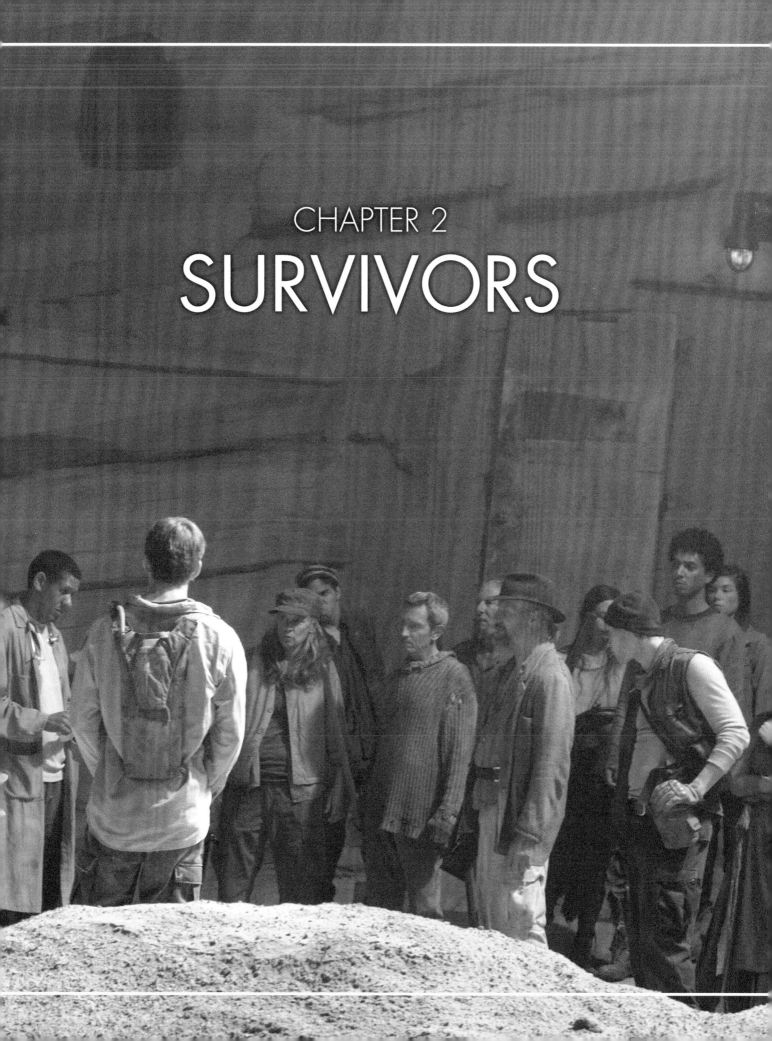

CHAPTER 2
SURVIVORS

Melanie fights off Seekers to avoid capture.

A cross the snowy fields of an arctic forest the young girl stalks game with bow and arrow— and a gun. Her father, an ex-intelligence operative and assassin, has trained her well. His little girl is adept at weapons and martial arts, her senses are finely sharpened, and her focus and willpower are indomitable. As Nick Wechsler sat in the dark movie theater and watched *Hanna* (the 2011 thriller directed by Joe Wright), he saw in the actress playing the title role exactly what they needed for Wanda/ Mel—someone able to play a complex character and also be physically active. Wechsler could barely wait for the end credits to head to the lobby, call his producing partners, and tell them he'd found their lead.

Saoirse Ronan had been on a list of thirty actresses being considered for *The Host* but was basically out of the running when Wechsler saw *Hanna.* Meyer had wanted an actress in her mid- to late twenties; Ronan was seventeen. The producers thought the part should be played by an American; Ronan was Irish. But in a whirlwind seventy-two hours, a script for *The Host* was in the hands of Ronan's agent and Wechsler was on the phone with Ronan's parents, and then, when Saoirse came on the line, he offered her the part.

"By the way," Wechsler added, "after writing the script, Andrew Niccol left our project to go make his film *In Time.* Our movie was still speculative at that point and *In Time* was Andrew's creation and ready to go. By the time Andrew was in post[production] on that movie, we were working with Inferno Entertainment to do international sales for *The Host*, and Stephenie and I put together a presentation for the Cannes Film Festival. I called Andrew and said, 'I'm going to Cannes to put this movie together and I've just put Saoirse Ronan in the lead. Do you want to come back on board and be the director?' And he said, 'Yeah.'" (Niccol says Ronan was one of the incentives

Ronan's performance and the film's visual style were key in portraying two characters within a single body.

for him to direct *The Host* and calls her "one of the most truthful actors on-screen today.")

Steve Schwartz recalled that during that limbo period when Niccol was off *The Host*, director Susanna White, whose features include *Jane Eyre* (2006), was briefly attached. "She had considered using effects in the portrayal of Wanda/Mel. With Andrew back at the helm, and with the attachment of Saoirse Ronan, performance was clearly the way to go. In Saoirse, we had a phenomenon. I believe she will be one of the greatest actresses of her generation—the next Meryl Streep."

"It was a joy to watch Saoirse Ronan work," said script supervisor Sam Sullivan. "For half the movie, [Wanda and Melanie's] conversations were inside their heads, so it was challenging to bring that out physically so we could see it. It was her voice talking to herself, and the way it was photographed. A lot of visual style went along with this duality. But she was so on it, you definitely got the sense of two different women in one body."

"The idea of two characters in one was actually really easy," Meyer observed. "Andrew, Nick, and I never really understood why that seemed so difficult to people. A lot of it is performance, and it was a bigger

Saoirse Ronan on set with her parents, Paul and Monica Ronan

worry before Saoirse came on board. Then we weren't worried about it anymore."

Saoirse Ronan (Saoirse is pronounced *sir-sha*) was born in New York, where her father began his acting career, and she grew up among his circle of actors, directors, writers, and theater friends. She was about five years old when her family moved back to Ireland, and seven when she made her acting debut—as a clown in a short film her father was making. "I wasn't too pleased—I did it because Dad asked me to, as a favor," Ronan said with a chuckle. "Later I went with his agent to put me up for a few things."

From a small role in the Irish drama *The Clinic*, Ronan moved on to an Oscar-nominated turn in Joe Wright's *Atonement* (2007), the part of the young girl

Saoirse Ronan as Wanda and (opposite page) as Melanie

who is murdered in Peter Jackson's *The Lovely Bones* (2009), and *Hanna*. "I think acting is a very personal thing and it's going to be different for everyone," she said in her soft, lyrical Irish accent. "Some actors have a technique. Others don't realize they have a technique, but they actually do. For me, I just naturally get to know my characters very well. I've always loved the films I've been a part of and really cared about the story. I'm always thinking about it, so it's a natural step to become that character."

The challenge in her dual character was bringing in a different physicality, accent, and mannerism for each. "There's a real contrast between them," Ronan said. "Wanda is your typical soul—very soft-spoken; she doesn't have any aggression, hatred, or negative emotions toward anyone. Although she inhabits a host from the States, Andrew and I didn't want her to have a modern, general American accent. She needed to have something otherworldly about her voice. We looked at actresses from the seventies, like Jane Fonda, and how they spoke, which is different from nowadays. As time moves on, people have different ways of speaking, different slang words. We wanted to go back to a more reserved, well-spoken young lady. Melanie has a mild southern accent and is very feisty. She's had to fight for a lot in her life. She's quite tough because she's had to take care of her brother, and that's given her a real

thick skin. I play Wanda more than Melanie, but I prefer Melanie because she's just lots of fun to play—she has a bit of bite to her."

With the casting of their lead, the production began putting together the rest of the cast, starting with a London casting session between Saoirse and actors auditioning for the role of Melanie's love interest, Jared.

Auditioning is a grinding process that often ends in disappointment. Even veteran actors endure the trial of investing their emotions in and sometimes even staking their careers on characters they can explore fully only by winning the part. They read from "sides," dialogue exchanges from select scenes,

The challenge in her dual character was bringing in a different physicality, accent, and mannerism for each.

not even full scripts. There can be a number of auditions before the final one, with the director, producers, casting director, and others intently watching every mannerism, gesture, and nuance. In the case of Jared, there was the added pressure of a romantic connection with the lead character. "They call it the chemistry test," said Max Irons, a twenty-six-year-old London-based actor who auditioned for Jared. "When I did *Red Riding Hood* a couple years ago, about eighteen of us boys were being cycled through, doing the same scene with [lead actress] Amanda Seyfried. And you've got the producers who just watch for that chemistry. We can't make it, we can't identify it, we can't really replicate it—you try, but you can't really. It's up to them if it's there or not."

Other than *Red Riding Hood* (2011) and some episodes of the TV series *The Runaway*, Irons, the son of actor Jeremy Irons and actress Sinéad Cusack, was focused on the stage. His professional stage debut in

Wallenstein, at the Chichester Festival Theatre in 2009, earned him a nomination for a prestigious Ian Charleson Award, a British theatrical award for young actors. But he read *The Host* script, sent an audition tape, and found himself acting with Ronan in front of Andrew Niccol. "You know when you have a good audition, and I did a good audition with Saoirse, I think we got that chemistry. It's hard not to, because there's something magic about her, something in her eyes. It's subtle. She has so much emotional maturity, and she was seventeen at the time of the audition."

Irons waited a month to learn if he had the part. Halfway through the wait, he saw a dispiriting news release listing the performers up for Jared. "They were all better-known than me, all physically muscular. I thought I was out of the running. Then, two weeks later, I got a phone call and I was over the moon!" (The production could have spared Irons his anxious wait. According to Wechsler, right after his audition, Niccol called and said, "This is it for Jared—this is the guy.")

Wanda and Ian

"Jake Abel has played the antagonist in a lot of movies, the tough, intimidating guy who gives someone a hard time. When we originally thought of Ian, we thought he should be more of a sensitive guy. How do you make believable someone who falls in love with an alien consciousness? Casting Jake was going against type—that was Andrew's gut call. He wanted to go against expectations."

—Nick Wechsler, producer

Abel and Ronan rest between takes.

The auditions moved to the United States, where Jake Abel was cast as Ian O'Shea, the cave dweller who falls in love with Wanda. Abel, who starred in *Percy Jackson & the Olympians: The Lightning Thief* (2010) and has appeared in such popular TV shows as *Grey's Anatomy* and *CSI: NY*, had known Ronan as one of the cast of *The Lovely Bones* and felt that this helped during their audition. "Saoirse and I get on very well—we're like best buds," Abel said. "Even though we worked so little together in *The Lovely Bones*, we had a past and felt comfortable together. And she's such a sweet person and so talented. It's not that difficult, honestly, to get along with Saoirse Ronan. I'd always looked forward to working with her again. If I just plant my feet in front of her and let go, we'll go somewhere. You

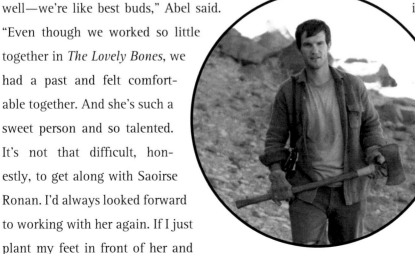

Lee Hardee as Aaron

don't always find that in young actors."

Many of the cave dwellers weren't as open-minded as Ian about having an alien in their midst. Such was Aaron, "one of the tight crew in the cave," noted Lee Hardee, who won the part after an audition in New Orleans. "It's like your thirtieth audition. You prepare the best you can. I didn't have the full script. You start off with sides, so you're trying to piece together what's actually going on. You do your best to interpret what's on the page and read as much as you can into it. Hopefully, you make the right choices. Then you wait and see what happens. Say a prayer."

Hardee has no illusions about the movie business. His only previous film experience was a small role in his first feature, *Jonah Hex*, that ended up on

William Hurt as Jeb Stryder

"It's a sort of post-alien holocaust story where the human race has been invaded, [but now] they have a relationship in which they begin to entertain wisdom from either side, as a choice, rather than the usual or natural choice, which would be to be antagonized and defensive."

—**William Hurt**, actor

the proverbial cutting-room floor, while a bigger role in a low-budget Screen Actors' Guild production was completed, but the film ran out of money in postproduction and was never released. Winning a part in *The Host* was a taste of the dream. "It's such a difficult and unstable industry, especially starting off," he reflected. "But as long as I can remember, all I've wanted to do is act. This is the passion."

Besides Wanda/Mel, the other key role was arguably that of Melanie's eccentric uncle, Jeb Stryder. In the novel, the crusty recluse discovers a huge cave and spends years adapting it for the doomsday scenario that actually comes to pass when aliens invade. Nick Wechsler had Jeff Bridges in mind for Jeb, but he wasn't available. "Then Andrew and I found out that William Hurt was available," Wechsler recalled, "and we thought, 'Wow, he's one of our favorite actors, and he hasn't been strip-mined.' He hasn't done a hundred movies in the last ten years, like some actors of his ilk. He's a bit of a recluse—I think he lives on a farm in Oregon and doesn't come out much, let's put it that way. I hadn't seen much of him since *A History of Violence* [the 2005 release for which Hurt was nominated for an Oscar]. I had no idea what to expect. We sent him the book and script and he flipped out! He really wanted this, and we respond to passion. He loved the themes, such as man's relationship to the planet and other species, and he loves science fiction. But everybody who we cast in this film loved the material and wanted to be part of it."

The cast bonded with a two-week rehearsal during which they broke down and worked through every scene. "We sat around a table every day and discussed the script and asked questions and figured things out, then we ate sushi, then we discussed the script for another four hours," Saoirse Ronan recalled. "I think it's always great to get to know the actors first, form

"I've always loved Jake as an actor. He steals the scene and you watch him instead of the people you're supposed to be watching. That is a quality Saoirse has as well, and one of the things we talked about was, 'How are we going to get guys on the screen that we are going to look at instead of Saoirse?' You know, people who can divert our attention even a little bit from what she's doing. And Jake has that quality and that presence."

—Stephenie Meyer

Jared and Ian discuss what to do about the alien in their midst.

a relationship and be comfortable with them. It was nice to have that, because when you're on a film and there's no rehearsal, you can sometimes feel like you've been thrown into the deep end and it takes a little bit longer to figure out."

Jake Abel said that he had never had that kind of rehearsal experience before. He added that the director welcomed everyone's contribution—unusual given that Niccol had such a strong, unified vision as both the screenwriter and the director. "Andrew separates himself as a writer and director in a way I've never seen. He'd refer to himself as the writer of the script, in the third person. He'd mention 'the drunk who's probably at the bar right now, writing the gibberish he writes.' He actually writes the most amazing material, but anytime we wanted to tweak something, he was willing to do it. He'd go, 'Oh, the writer—what was he thinking!' He doesn't hold it so precious that no one

can have their own ideas. And the actors on this film all came with their own ideas."

An actor's character is conjured through performance but also through costume, hair, makeup, props, lighting, and camerawork. Just as the actors broke down the script, so too did production department heads, including costume designer Erin Benach, whose wardrobe would be an intrinsic part of the world. "We imagined the setting by taking the present day, but if the occupation started tomorrow, the movie would pick up ten years down the road," explained Benach, whose recent credits include *Drive* (2011). "In terms of technology, everything is pretty much present-day, except that in those ten years the souls have built monuments and structures that represent their society. In this movie, more than others, we had a concept of what everything was going to be before I even started working with the actors. By the

Max Irons as Jared Howe

"Filmmaking is a director's medium. For the writer, everything is possible, but the director has to adapt to reality. It's why I generally keep the writer off the set. He's too precious. To amuse myself, I often talk about the writer in the third person. The duality of the roles [writer/director] was even more apparent on this movie, where we have an actress playing two characters. In fact, we gave Saoirse two chairs on set—one for Wanderer and one for Melanie."

—**Andrew Niccol**, director

time I was meeting with actors, I could say, 'This is how we're putting the world together.' They'd want to have something for their character, whatever it might be, and I'd put it together with what we figured out. It was very synergistic."

An irony of soul society is that the souls invade planets and possess bodies, but their ultimate goal is to make each world better. Soul nature is peaceful, passive, and orderly, and their medical technology has vanquished disease and injury. Even the Seekers, charged with keeping order, do not fit the classic description of "bad guys," Benach felt. Seekers wear black in the novel, but Benach and the director decided that dressing them in white worked better. "Andrew and I had a lot of early discussions about the mentality of the Seekers and their motivation. They're trying to create peace on Earth—that's their whole goal. I felt a sea of aliens dressed in black wouldn't be accurate as to why they're there."

For the humans, the director wanted a paramilitary theme, the look of embattled freedom fighters. The humans also venture into occupied territory to get supplies and need to dress like souls to blend in (they wear dark glasses to hide their lack of a ring around the pupils of their eyes, the telltale sign of a possessed human). "The soul look is very tailored, a little bit from the 1930s and '40s, but in the end the idea is you can't tell the era," Benach explained. "It's a style you haven't really seen before, although it's clothing you'd recognize—it's a sweater, shirt, pants. It's what's left on Earth, but tweaked and put together in a way you don't normally see, just to get the sense this isn't normal human society."

By Christmas 2011, Candy Neal was figuring out Saoirse Ronan's hair. After a flurry of phone calls and e-mails between her and Niccol, it was decided to make a wig for the actress. "And of course you can't go to

"I thought it was interesting to have a sci-fi film where for once the aliens are not necessarily the bad guys. Yes, we're being invaded and taken over by the souls, but in a way they perfect our world, they perfect the human flaws, and yet the human mind and the human spirit is so strong that even the souls have difficulty overcoming that."

—Diane Kruger, actor

The souls' costumes are tailored, with elements from the thirties, forties, and fifties (left). Jared and Ian must dress like souls when they go out on supply raids (right).

just any wigmaker," Neal noted. "You have to go to the best wigmaker. Saoirse would be wearing the wig every day, and there was going to be a lot of action in this movie."

The wigmaker was Natascha Ladek of Favian Wigs in Los Angeles. Ronan was back home, so Neal had a hair stylist in Ireland make a Saran wrap mold of Ronan's head, which the wigmaker used to custom-design a wig to fit Ronan. Neal created a booklet of potential hair colors for the director to consider. Three weeks after that, a blond wig was ready. By then, principal photography was approaching and cast and crew were starting their prep work in

> "Saoirse is an amazing actress. She has been working really hard on set. I admire her for that. Whenever she walks into a room, everyone just starts smiling."
>
> —Chandler Canterbury, actor

Baton Rouge, where Candy and Natascha flew to meet Ronan for a fitting. Two weeks later, Ve Neill arrived and there were tests with hair, makeup, and wardrobe.

The weekend before the first day of shooting, Neal got a call from Niccol. He began with the ominous words, "You know, I'm really concerned ..."

Saoirse, a natural blonde, had come to the production with red hair from a previous movie. Niccol thought the blond wig looked beautiful but felt there wasn't enough of a family resemblance with Chandler Canterbury, the brown-haired actor playing her younger brother, Jamie. "So he asked, 'What

> "It's not just about makeup, or hair, or the wardrobe alone—it's all of it, together. You're creating a look. Ve [Neill] and I often discuss how she's going to do the makeup, and then I'll go see the wardrobe, and that's how I come up with my ideas. And Andrew certainly has ideas, and so do the actors."
>
> —Candace "Candy" Neal, hair department head

can we do?' We thought about coloring the wig, but decided to move away from wigs," Neal recalled. "This all came down on a Saturday, and we were to start shooting on Monday. So we had to move quickly."

At the eleventh hour, Neal went to Sally's, a beauty supply store in Baton Rouge that provided machine-made hair extensions to be used for Saoirse's look. "We didn't have time to do anything else," Neal explained. "We put blond highlights in Chandler's hair, because it was so dark, and took the red out of Saoirse's hair. I had David [Blair], my assistant, dye the extensions a medium brown, a chestnut color, and clip them in. Everybody loved it, and that was Saoirse's look. After months and months of preparation, Andrew went in a whole different direction. But she was the most important character, so we had to get her look nailed down. And that's how movies are made!"

"It all comes from the director," added Ve Neill, whose makeup for *Beetlejuice* (1988), *Mrs. Doubtfire* (1993), and *Ed Wood* (1994) won her Academy Awards. "You have to have a good rapport and find out exactly what he's looking for in the characters. I thought the wardrobe [for the Seekers] was very utilitarian-looking and that it would be great to give them a really clean, soft look. I recall we did the first [test] look on Diane. I used Kid, an eye-shadow color by MAC, in the crease of her eye, an almost creamy caramel color that shapes the eye to make it look pretty and soft. Then I added a thin coat of mascara to define the eye, but no more than that. The souls don't spend a lot of time doing

Chandler Canterbury plays Melanie's younger brother, Jamie Stryder.

anything to themselves—they're sort of perfect on their own. I didn't think about it that long—it just seemed that was what their look should be, and Andrew loved it. My test makeup day was actually the day they shot the teaser, so I'm glad he liked it!"

In contrast to the harmony and perfection of soul society are the bedraggled survivors in the desert cave. "They've been living in caves for years, and their clothes are tattered and torn," Neal noted. "They harvest their own wheat and make their own food and probably stitch together and patch their own clothing.

The human survivors wear costumes that reflect their hardscrabble existence.

Their life is twenty-four hours a day how they're going to survive.

"The humans are more organic," Neill added. "They don't spend a lot of time making themselves up, but they frequently go into town and steal things here and there. The girls have a little makeup, nothing glamorous. It's more of leftover makeup they put on to try and stay a little feminine. The guys don't clean-shave themselves every day, so they have a bit of a rugged look. I didn't really use foundation on the men, only on Max, because we had him a little tanned from the beginning of the film. Jake had a little something around the eyes, usually a liquid dirt you rub into the skin to give an aged quality,

Diane Kruger as the Seeker

like a patina. Everybody is what I call 'teched down.' They don't look smudgy and dirty, but they don't look spanking clean either. They have an edge—they look lived-in, more or less."

The costume department, which had up to fifteen people working during the busy period leading up to principal photography, took charge of distressing the humans' clothes. "We had an ager/dyer working a month in advance of filming," Benach explained. "We imagine what activities the person who wears the clothes might be engaged in. You might wash the clothes in chemicals to break down fibers so they're softer and more malleable and will lie on the body a certain way. We'll take sandpaper bars and rough up patches where people would lean against things. We make the garment look and feel like it's been lived in for many, many years. You're giving a history and personality to the garment by physically altering it."

Melanie is first introduced in her postinvasion "runaway outfit," as Benach called it. "We needed a Mel versus a Wanda feel. In flashbacks, we have Mel being a little tough, but also feminine and a little innocent. Her wardrobe always has this kind of tomboy twist to it. She's a survivor, the caretaker and protector of her little brother. Then, when she's captured and given the soul of Wanda, you see her eyes change and she wears a wardrobe from the soul people. Wanda has

Max Irons as Jared

a very simple and symmetrical uniform we built that has a kind of forties sweater and fifties pants, a pastel outfit with happy colors. The sweater top fastened with fabric-covered buttons down the back, was tapered along the bodice, and fitted at the shoulders and loosely draped at the breast."

Benach added that William Hurt was happy with what she had in mind for Jeb Stryder. "The idea is he was one of the first to be living in the desert. He found this cave and was developing it years before the occupation started. He's out in the West, in the middle of nowhere. It was the feeling that he was kind of a cowboy and this was his world. It just fit."

Candy Neal recalled that when Hurt came on, he

Ronan's costumes help mark the distinction between Melanie and Wanda.

"William Hurt as Jeb has a great look—he kind of reminds me of Indiana Jones. The cave is his place and the people are invited there by him. If they mess up they're asked to leave and have to fend for themselves, so everybody pretty much does what he says."

—**Ve Neill**, makeup department head

had already begun transforming himself. "William is meticulous about how he wants to look. He gives it a lot of thought, way before he starts a film. When I came on he had already started growing his hair and had pulled it back into a little bit of a ponytail, and that made perfect sense."

"I think William grew his beard on his own, but that was something he and Andrew discussed," Ve Neill added. "The only thing we really altered was they wanted him to look a bit younger, so I colored his beard every day to give him more of a youthful appearance. For a character that isn't really well groomed, [Jeb] keeps his hair and beard pretty tidy and he's not filthy. His clothes are aged, but they're still very well put together."

For Frances Fisher's Maggie, Neal again called upon Natascha. There wasn't the time or the budget left to custom-design a new wig. Based on what Neal wanted, the wigmaker pulled from her stock. Fisher wasn't scheduled to be on set at the start of principal photography, so shooting was under way when the actress had her fittings in Los Angeles. The test photos were e-mailed to the production team in Louisiana, where the director, producers, and Neal discussed the options. "We narrowed down to one look, and Natascha made adjustments on that wig," Neal explained. "I received the wig, Frances flew out, and the next day we started shooting with her."

Fisher recalls that when Niccol first called, he asked if she'd mind playing a white-haired old woman. "Andrew asked, 'Are you willing not to look elegant?'" Fisher said with a smile. "I said, 'Yeah, of course. I'm an actress.' I went to Natascha, who is famous for doing wigs. I tried on a bunch and I liked this one. It wasn't quite white; it looked natural. I figured we've been living in the caves for ten years, so even if I once dyed my hair, hair dye is very low on the list of necessities."

Frances Fisher as
Maggie Stryder

Inimitable touches were added to the characters by the props department, headed by Guillaume Delouche. "We're responsible for anything the actors touch or interact with, or any object that has a particular action in the film," explained the prop master, who recently worked on *Abraham Lincoln: Vampire Hunter.* "We'll integrate with other departments, like the art department, set dressing, effects, stunts. If actors have a particular action that requires stunts, we would do props for that stunt, such as make something out of soft rubber as opposed to steel. It's a very neat way to collaborate on a picture."

Delouche worked on *The Truman Show* and knew Niccol from that production, but this was his first assignment with Niccol as director. "It's always very interesting to work with a new director. You have to learn someone's process, and once you're in the fray of a production, it's just working with it. It's fascinating because you get a privileged seat to see someone's brain at work. Every director's style is different. Andrew is extremely exacting, like a surgeon. You might do two or three versions of something and

"The great thing on this picture was we had two worlds. You had this beautiful idyllic universe where the souls are evolving and everything is perfect and everyone is beautiful, clean, and polite. And then you have this postapocalyptic world in the cave, where they take items and try to make them work again, like old farm tools and old guns."

—Guillaume Delouche, prop master

Two key props were a modern handgun and an old-fashioned rifle.

then go, 'Oh, yes, now I get the train of thought.' He's definitely not a shortcut type of person, so it keeps you on your toes."

Guns were among the key props. "Andrew was very specific with the guns," Delouche explained. "It would have been easy to create a human army with assault rifles and lots of hardware, but that would take away from the novel. We looked for rifles from a bygone era, things with wood grips and wood stocks and blued steel. The only time we went a little fancy was when we made a pair of costume Glocks with silver slides. Andrew liked the duotone look, so we have the tell-tale black polymer Glock frame, and we found beautiful nitrate slides to put in. We blanked them, and that's one of the hero guns of the movie. But everything else is pretty classic. The idea is that the souls have destroyed all stockpiles of modern weaponry, so you have what you could grab. It was a big-time survival thing we had to translate."

The props department (which, like costume,

"The gun is Uncle Jeb's badge of authority—he's the constable of the group."

makes, buys, or rents what it needs) bought a classic twelve-gauge, over-under trap shotgun for Jeb. The gun was aged, with a brown leather sling added for carrying the weapon, and a rubber version was made for stunt scenes. "The gun is Uncle Jeb's badge of authority—he's the constable of the group," Delouche said. "All other guns we see are outside the confines of the cave. The underlying story is that there was probably a problem early on with people packing guns in the compound. Jeb now doesn't allow anyone to carry weapons; he's the only one who's allowed to. That made a lot of sense."

Making sure everyone was aware of what was going on at any point during filming was script supervisor Sam Sullivan's job. The challenge of continuity, as with virtually all productions, was that the screenplay was filmed out of sequence. A scene shot on the stage at Baton Rouge might continue at an exterior location in New Mexico weeks later. On set, Sullivan always had a big book with him—the screenplay, jam-packed with notes, particularly for editor Tom Nordberg. "Every time we do a scene, I'll show how many takes we've done, what cameras we've used. I'll make notes like 'This is Andrew's favorite take,' or 'Don't use this take because the gun is in the left hand, but it's supposed to be in the right.' I like writing it down. I'm old school. If I write it down, I know it's in the book.

"The actors are a big part of what I do," Sullivan added. "I try to make sure they're looking right and are informed of things that happen before and after a scene. I see that they are wearing the right clothes and saying the right words, that they have the right props, that the room is dressed the right way. I coordinate with hair, makeup, props, set dressing, camera, sound—I'm in the middle of the hub, a department of one. I like to be close by, so if an actor forgets their line, I can throw them dialogue when they need it. For example, the character of Wanda has different [physical] tics from Melanie, and I might need to remind Andrew and the cast about that. This is a big movie, but it has a very actor-friendly feel. Andrew was very conscious of giving the actors space to find the scene first, and then we'd shoot it."

Paul Olinde, a veteran of over sixty films, most recently *Abraham Lincoln: Vampire Hunter*, was gaffer, meaning that he was in charge of lighting and worked directly with Roberto Schaefer. "The look of the movie is his responsibility, so I light the movie for him. With each DP you have a different task in achieving the look, lighting-wise. For this movie, the lighting is pretty traditional. We wanted the movie to look real, so that you believe all of it is real. The trick for us, and for most films, was to light it so an audi-

Wanda awakens in her apartment (top). Jake Abel as Ian (center). The Seeker interviews Wanda (bottom).

The Louisiana State Museum in Baton Rouge serves as the exterior of the Soul Center (left). Wanda visits the Soul Center, escorted by a Seeker (right).

ence never notices the movie is lit by anything other than a natural source, such as sunlight or lamps. You always want to have a justification for a light source. The goal is for an audience never to think about lighting. If the audience notices the lighting, you've failed. It should look natural."

With wintry weather in New Mexico, it was an easy call to kick off principal photography in Baton Rouge in February. Even exterior locations in Louisiana were shot toward that end of the schedule, when it was warmer. "The shoot was supposed to be fifty-five days, but they cut five days out," Roberto Schaefer noted. "So we had to cram fifty-five days into fifty." The filming schedule was set for thirty-six days in Louisiana, some time for travel, and fourteen days in New Mexico.

The shooting stages did not come easily. New Orleans had productions occupying every soundstage and hotel room and all the local craftsmen. Baton Rouge was similarly busy, with most of its local craftspeople engaged on other productions. Shreveport had converted warehouses to film in but had no practical locations that anyone liked. Seemingly the only option was to do the stage work in Shreveport, then catch exteriors in Baton Rouge and New Orleans. "Luckily, at the eleventh hour, one of the big movies at Celtic Studios in Baton Rouge fell apart and the other, a Tom Cruise movie, released a stage," Ray Angelic said. "So, based on one available stage, we made the decision to pull up stakes and leave Shreveport. Even though we hadn't landed there yet, we walked away from deposits and made it a Baton Rouge–New Orleans movie."

Locations in Baton Rouge included the Louisiana State Museum, the Shaw Center for the Arts, and an abandoned big-box store, which the production converted into a multipurpose filming and production facility. The locations in New Orleans ranged from a new cancer center under construction to neighborhoods representing the soul world, as well

> "Making a movie is a big puzzle. If you keep remembering what the whole picture is supposed to look like, the pieces fit together better."
>
> —Sam Sullivan, script supervisor

as swampland for flashback scenes.

The available stage in Baton Rouge was Stage 8, Celtic's biggest, where the production had to build its cave set. "Building a cave set wasn't unique," Angelic noted. "But making one that looked realistic and fit Andrew's vision would be a challenge on any film. But since Louisiana was completely swamped with other movies—no pun intended—we had to bring in lots of art department people and

Canterbury and Ronan are prepped for a flashback scene.

construction crew. We did get some terrific local crew—we just couldn't get many of them. We also had a very compressed prep time for a film this size."

"Anytime you try to design and build that big a natural complex, like a cave system, and make it seem like it's *not* been done on a stage, it requires a lot of craft in terms of production design, lighting, and cinematography," added Nick Wechsler. "Yeah, we were nervous about it."

Seekers approach a house in search of human survivors.

CHAPTER 3
THE CAVE

As the invaders remake the human world into a perfect reflection of their innate sense of order, the humans dwelling in Jeb's cave try to keep a semblance of civilization alive. Production designer Andy Nicholson calls the cave "the HQ of the human resistance." In the novel and the movie, the cave includes a main cavern, individual living spaces, a kitchen and eating area, an infirmary, an underground river and bathing area, a field for planting, even a mirror system for catching and distributing light. The colony (as it is called in the novel) even has vehicles, including Unimogs, the multipurpose four-wheel-drive Mercedes-Benz trucks perfect for desert terrain and raids on soul cities.

There had to be a rationale for everything in the cave, a logic extending from design to set construction. Nicholson was concerned that the layout be clear, so audiences would always know where they were. "I had a lot of conversations with Andrew about how to move spatially from one location to the other, how that would work with the characters and audience. For example, in movies with houses and rooms, subliminally you're set up so you know when you're heading for a scary place. I thought it was important to have different parts of the cave the audience could easily identify so they'd know where they were. To help with

"I thought it was important to have different parts of the cave the audience could easily identify so they'd know where they were."

Unimogs are used to bring supplies back to the human colony. Kyle, Jared, and Brandt gear up for a raid.

Jeb shows Wanda the underground river (top). Cave tunnels have distinctive shapes and lighting (bottom left). Jared keeps a vigil outside Wanda's room (bottom right).

that, tunnels connecting different rooms were designed with specific shapes, whether natural or carved out." Examples were the carved corridor to Wanda's cell, natural formations in the river and bathing pool areas, and passageways connecting to the main cave area that included both natural and man-made formations.

Nicholson's art department began developing a low-resolution 3-D mock-up of the cave interior, a virtual world that allowed a fly-through with the virtual camera. "I knew how big the main cave could be, because I knew the stage we had in Baton Rouge," Nicholson explained. "You do a dry run with a flying camera through virtual spaces. Then it's about turning that virtual space into a physical set."

The low-resolution environment evolved as the design team and director worked out everything from

The cave interior was first rendered in a low-resolution 3-D mock-up (above), then given color and texture (top). (Opposite page) Irons and Ronan in the Cathedral Cave.

spatial dynamics and surface textures to areas where greenscreens would be integrated into the physical set, enabling visual effects to extend the cave's dimensions. "We take the limitations of the stages and give them a boost," visual effects supervisor/producer Ellen Somers said of the CG work that would fill the greenscreen spaces. "We lend a volume of space that could not be affordable, or practical, on even the most generous of soundstages."

To keep it visually interesting, Nicholson added a line of strata running at a fifteen-degree angle. The conceptual phase climaxed with a high-definition model that was sliced up into scaled sections—"templates," Nicholson called them—that served as virtual blueprints the construction department could build from.

"An unbelievable amount of credit has to be given to Tom Morris, our construction coordinator, a position that often goes unrecognized," said executive producer Ray Angelic. "They're the guys who, under Andy Nicholson's direction, made that whole vision of the cave come to life. Tom was incredibly successful, I think, in pulling off this task where there were very

"The sets are phenomenal. The interior cave, which is in the soundstage, is massive. The first time you walk in—I won't forget my first reaction—you're in awe. Your jaw drops. These locations are movie magic. When you're a kid and you go to Universal Studios or Disneyland and you ride the rides, it's that. Saoirse and I talked about that. It's got that same magic feeling."

—Jake Abel, actor

few local hires available, and getting it done in time and on budget."

Ray Angelic described the immensity of what was built on Stage 8. "As you rolled up the overhead door and entered, you were looking at our giant hero cave and smaller caves. The stage was about twenty-eight thousand square feet, and almost every inch was the set we built off from the fire lanes. We built about three-quarters, and a quarter was greenscreen."

There was also a "wild" element, a massive curved rock wall section on wheels that was twenty-six feet wide and twenty feet tall. The movable piece had several nicknames, including "tsunami" and "tornado," but was usually called "the pork chop." "Sometimes you don't want a huge cave to look at," Nicholson explained. "We could use the wild piece to squash down space and give perspective. You could place a camera in one place, roll the wall in, and it'd be like you were in a different cave. It gave us a more dynamic environment."

The set also had to match the sandstone textures of New Mexico. "You're dealing with a set made of foam or plaster that's painted," Nicholson said. "Most of the color in sandstone comes from sand. We ended up doing a lot of color finishes with sand on top of plaster, sprayed in at the last minute before the plaster set. It became tricky because you had to apply the paint in very thin washes. If you applied thick amounts, it just looked like a painted set no matter how much sand texture was in it. It took a lot of time to get to something that could work both close to camera and two hundred feet away."

The main space, dubbed the "Cathedral Cave," was the "social center of the Resistance's community," Nicholson wrote in his production notes.[4] For practical purposes, the main cave would be redressed as the colony's wheat field, making for a set more than two hundred feet long. "The challenge with any cave setting," Andrew Niccol explained, "is that it's generally not possible to shoot in a real cave. The work was compounded by having a wheat field and a river in the cave. The field in the cave is my favorite image from Stephenie's book, although the crop in the novel is corn. Every strand of wheat in a two-hundred-foot-long field had to be individually wired in place" by the greens department.

The props department played a part in the wheat field. "We really went the distance to show a little chain factory process of the colonists making baked goods," Delouche explained. "We supplied tools to make bread, and the various stages of preparation. Anything the actors interacted with, such as food, was made by us. Obviously, we had to make sure the food was hygienic and tasted good. We also had to check with cast members to see if they were allergic to anything, like gluten."

The wheat field had scenes of workers harvesting and dialogue with characters walking through the field. The camera crew had to get their shots across the vast space, and without crushing the wheat by laying down dolly tracks or even having a Steadicam operator moving through the fields. "I figured we had to glide over the wheat field," Roberto Schaefer said. "We were originally trying to get a fifty-foot [telescopic] Technocrane on a track for the big cave set, but I realized a fifty-footer would really do nothing in that big space. An Akela Crane or Strada Crane is sixty to one hundred feet long, but we couldn't use either

"Today's miracles are tomorrow's expectations."

—George "Bubba" Sheffield, key grip

Ian and Wanda take a water break while working in the wheat field.

system because it has a fixed arm and arcs and it requires enough room to move."

Schaefer learned that Chapman, a well-known maker of camera equipment for film and television productions, had a new seventy-three-foot telescopic camera arm that had been used only on a few commercials. It was called the Chapman Leonard Hydrascope. "The seventy-three-footer was for these sweeping and retracting shots in the wheat field, going along with the actors as they're walking and talking and pulling back and never touching the wheat at all," Schaefer explained. "Nick [Mastandrea], the first AD [assistant director], dubbed it 'the Titanic' because it's a large piece, with amazing steelwork. It has a stabilized head and almost no flexing, bouncing, or unnecessary movement. It's pretty impressive."

"I'll say this is death from above," key grip

Key grip George "Bubba" Sheffield

George "Bubba" Sheffield said with a grin. "This is the first show to have the seventy-three-foot Hydrascope. Because of these environments, this is what we ordered to help accommodate the shoot. I've been using this equipment for thirty years; I've seen it evolve and grow. As time has gone by, we've described shots we need and Leonard [Chapman, the company owner] has actually designed some things. I've had a fantastic relationship with the Chapmans for years, and they're staying up with the technology."

Rigging the cameras and setting up the greenscreens—the biggest being a 30-by-160-foot section, and twenty to thirty smaller setups—was the charge of Sheffield's grip department. "The challenge for us was interpreting what the production needs. If they say, 'We need a light in the air,' it's my job to figure out how to get the light in the air. We're in charge of

The seventy-three-foot Chapman Leonard Hydrascope allowed the crew to shoot across a vast space.

the movement of the camera, the safety of the set, the diffusion of light. If you need a camera mounted, it's the grip department's job to figure out how to do it. For the camera crane we have certain areas we attach it to so in case the camera has some type of catastrophic failure it won't fall on anybody. We make our camera mounts as we go, because there are so many variations of our shots. We'll build [camera] platforms from scratch; we'll attach it to the body of a vehicle and safety it from there. It's kind of liquid. We manufacture as we go—we have a forty-eight-foot trailer full of equipment for that.

"I've been doing this since the late eighties," Sheffield added. "You might have a team together with two hundred to three hundred years' worth of experience—it helps quite a bit! Buddy Carr, my dolly grip, is extremely important. Buddy is a legend. He works with camera, he's side by side with them all the time, and he's pretty much my

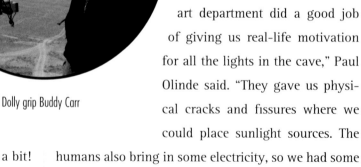

Dolly grip Buddy Carr

conduit to the director of photography. I've been with Roberto for a little over three years; we've done features and commercials. That experience really helps— it keeps you in tune with one another. Roberto and I talk quite a bit. We have to go over the schedule, the daily call sheet, because things change so fast and we have to be prepared for the next day. A lot of times we'll have late-night phone calls and conversations for things that are changing."

An important part of the set design was factoring in believable light sources. "The art department did a good job of giving us real-life motivation for all the lights in the cave," Paul Olinde said. "They gave us physical cracks and fissures where we could place sunlight sources. The humans also bring in some electricity, so we had some practical fluorescent lighting. It was always important for us to make sure the lights we used had a reasonable source in the world."

A massive mirror system was designed to bring light to the caves from the outside (above). Wanda and Ian use the practical wheel to angle the mirrors down (right).

A major justification for lighting was a mirror system built to catch sunlight and distribute it across the wheat field and caverns. The mirror system design became more refined as the art department thought about the moving pieces—winches and pulleys and brackets—that would be part of the physical set. "We used that as a starting point for the design and how it worked," said Nicholson. "It wasn't a massive structure. The parts were small enough and it was believable that you could get up there and fix them. The mirrors are different sizes and the metal holding them up is rusty. It's not perfect, but it works."

At one point in the story, a Seeker helicopter is heard and the mirrors have to be moved so glints of light aren't glimpsed from outside. "In an emergency, the humans can crank and winch the mirrors away so the sun's reflections can't be seen by the Seek-ers," Olinde explained. "The mirror will be digital, but we had to create light to look as if it were refracting off them. That was our most challenging task on the movie. We had a pretty big lighting truss with sixteen robotic lights, so when they cranked the winches and moved the mirrors, lights shaped as mirrors swept across the wheat field. The lighting unit itself was remote controlled and programmed to tilt, spin, focus, and do everything."

"They call these moving lights 'intelligent lights,'" Roberto Schaefer added. "You'll find them used in rock shows and stage shows. They can move and refocus, change colors, do all sorts of stuff. The actors would get over to the [practical] wheels and start pulling on these chains, you got a cue for 'lights,' and they had to be moved and timed at that point. We programmed the moving lights to simulate giant mirror reflections moving across the wheat field, up the sides of the cave walls, and disappearing as the sunlight is cut. We had a lighting dimmer board and a moving light-board operator, a pro who had done a lot of live shows. In fact, he had just come off a show in New Orleans where he had three thousand moving lights at one time. We just had sixteen lights, so it was pretty simple for him."

The cave had so many elements that the production also used another stage. Although soundstage space in Baton Rouge was at a premium, the produc-

tion found an abandoned store it used for a construction mill and the special effects shop. The "Super Store Stage," as it was called, included the underground river set, which had to look elemental and dangerous, and the serene and private bathing pool set. As Nicholson described the river in his production notes: "Based on Arizona slot canyons, passages in this set curve back and forth dramatically, the river and waterfall is a brutally swift current rushing through the set (sfx [special effects] pumped around 8,500 gals per sec). To fall [into the surging waters] had to feel fatal."

"The biggest challenge was the river and waterfall set that had to be built indoors," said Jack Lynch, the special effects coordinator. "It was figuring how to build the set and make it work with pumps and everything, how much flow rate the director wanted to see, the waterfalls, basically figuring out how it all would work."

"The river turned out to be a major engineering feat," Niccol added. "We needed to pump thousands of gallons of water every minute to create convincing rapids. The trick was to recycle the water and to fool

The cave set included an underground river (above). Wanda tries to keep Kyle from falling into the rapids (right).

the eye. The audience can't tell if a river is twenty feet deep or two feet deep, so we made it two feet."

For the individual living spaces, Nicholson's art department researched a similar dry cave environment: underground mines in Australia where miners lived and worked. "It turned out they really didn't do a lot to their underground living spaces," Nicholson explained. "They might paint the walls, but a lot of time they didn't because it's rock and there's dampness to worry about. People would just move in furniture. I did want Ian's room to look different, because there were a lot of scenes there. I came up with the idea of whitewashing the whole room because it got away from the brown. It worked great, because we also had shafts of light bouncing around in there."

Jake Abel felt at home in his character's room. "When I went into Ian's room there were tons of books, paintings he's taken from raids, a guitar. Ian is a bit innocent and sensitive, but he's also thoughtful and really intelligent. He's not afraid to protect the people he loves, whether it's his brother [Kyle] or Wanda or whoever. He's kind of complex in that

Ian shows Wanda his room.

Jared questions Wanda about her motives.

way and that was a lot of fun to explore."

One of the plot twists is that as Melanie longs for Jared, Wanda realizes that Ian is falling in love with her—and the feeling is mutual. "It's the 'interspecies relationship,' as Andrew Niccol told me before auditioning," Jake Abel said with a smile. "I knew I liked Ian, but I didn't know about playing him until talking to Andrew. He said what fascinated him about Ian is that he's so evolved, he can see beyond the enemy. He learns that *it* is not as bad as we think. And then *it* becomes a *she,* and the interspecies

"The chemistry with Max and Saoirse was just unbelievable and he's very expressive. He's able to do so much without saying a word, which is really impressive."

—Stephenie Meyer

thing no longer applies. It's one single entity Ian falls in love with. As an actor, you've got to know where you're coming from, what life in the cave and survival is, and what it means to have this vile enemy that wants to extinguish us brought into the cave, alive, which has never happened. The things I've experienced from Wanda slowly start to fissure my shell and break through."

Max Irons acknowledged that some fans of the novel didn't like his character. When Melanie is taken into the cave and Jared realizes his lost love is now possessed by

Jared reacts with shock and anger to the arrival of an alien in his beloved's body.

a soul, he lashes out. "The first scene she comes back, I hit her! I was worried about that scene because I hadn't quite got it in my head what it was really about. But it's not anger—it's pain, raw emotion. Your heart is saying it's still her, she looks and sounds the same, but the emotional part of your brain is saying you have to kill her! It's a struggle. So I never looked at him badly. I just thought he was the product of the life happening around him. As an actor you have to identify with the character, and Jared is a guy under extraordinary circumstances. What are his wants, needs, and fears? And those things change from scene to scene, from moment to moment. But they're relatively accessible if you understand the greater scheme of things—we're the last members of our race. You have to identify those things and get into that head space. He's violent and angry and [in the case of Wanda/Mel] one of the last to see the real soul beneath."

"What fascinated me about Jared and the world he lives in is that essentially the human race has died out. As far as we know, we're the last remaining few. When Jared lost Melanie, he hardened himself. He became a soldier. Then the specter of the girl he knew comes back into his life, but she's somebody else, an alien. He's a man who has gone through huge amounts of pain—everybody has."

—**Max Irons**, actor

Mustafa Harris, who plays Brandt, came to the production with his own backstory for his character. "I came up with a few things—it helps you along the way with your performance. I think Brandt lost someone in the transition of the humans losing Earth and the aliens taking it. Possibly he lost his family and wants to start a new one. Maybe in the cave he has a girlfriend—something that gives him a reason to keep going. I imagine it would be hard to keep motivated when you're living underground in a cave. His motivation is he feels like one day we could actually win this, we could get our planet back.

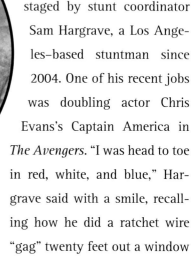

Mustafa Harris as Brandt

"One day you're shooting one scene, the next day you're shooting another," Harris added. "You learn to use whatever tools you need to get you where you need to be. You learn to morph into the day's work, to get there mentally. For me, it's just a quiet reminder of what has happened and where we are. I try to put out of my mind what I know is going to happen and be mindful of where I am and the scene we're shooting. It's challenging because there's always so much going on. The shot is being set up, you have to have a certain prop, you have to remember to hit a certain mark, and, oh, you also have to perform! It just becomes a weird combination of clearing your mind and homing in."

Many cave scenes crackle with the tension of having an alien dwelling within and the fear that Wanda will lead the Seekers to the colonists. That tension erupts in several fight scenes, which were among the action choreographed and staged by stunt coordinator Sam Hargrave, a Los Angeles–based stuntman since 2004. One of his recent jobs was doubling actor Chris Evans's Captain America in *The Avengers*. "I was head to toe in red, white, and blue," Hargrave said with a smile, recalling how he did a ratchet wire "gag" twenty feet out a window and smashed onto a car roof, then did ten takes of the star-spangled superhero leaping from a bridge onto a stationary bus on a gold tail wire rig that controlled his landing.

A dividend of modern filmmaking is that wires and safety rigging can be digitally removed from the film, allowing repeated takes of exciting action with a high safety factor. "It's not all just put your mouthpiece in and do it," Hargrave said. "You can use camera tricks

"The fighting style Andrew wanted for the humans was very basic. These guys are survivors, not martial artists or special forces kind of guys. Their fight scenes were big right hands and trying to choke people, lots of basic, primal moves."

—**Sam Hargrave**, stunt coordinator

Jared squares off against Kyle, Ian, and Brandt.

and wires to make things easier and safer. We're not daredevils, we're stunt professionals. I'm trying to be like some of the guys I came up with, like Tim Rigby, R. A. Rondell, or David Leitch. They are good communicators, very organized, and push the envelope of action while keeping everyone safe and happy."

Hargrave had done stunt coordinating for music videos and low-budget and "no budget" films, but *The Host* was his first major stunt coordinating job, thanks to the recommendation of stunt coordinator and second unit director David Leitch, who had been asked to do *The Host* but wasn't available. A stunt coordinator often leads a team that helps plot the action, but Hargrave was flying solo, although he had riggers for wirework and hired stunt performers as needed. "On this show it was just me, so I'd have it in my head. I'd be alone in my hotel room, just throwing kicks and punches in the air on one side, then switch to the other side. It was a good challenge. I'd first talk with the director, because he was very specific about what he wanted to see. Then I'd work with the actors."

One of the cave fights pitted Max Irons's Jared against Mustafa Harris's Brandt. "I didn't need to double them—they were both physically capable actors," Hargrave noted. "As a safety precaution, we laid down one-inch foam mats so they had the freedom to go hard. They were rolling around and fighting on the ground, which can get ugly if actors don't work well together or they're not physically capable. Fighting for film is more like dancing than fighting. You have a partner and a rhythm you work with. You can't fight *against* your partner. You have to work with him but make it look like you're fighting."

In another scene, Kyle, played by Boyd Holbrook, attempts to kill Wanda by the river. The struggle takes them to the edge of the waterfall. Kyle hits his head and almost falls in. "Boyd was great—he's a very physically capable actor. We had him on a safety cable and put the camera in a favorable position to sell the idea of him hitting his head against the rock wall. The cable gave him the freedom to go as big as he wanted and know he was always going to be stopped at a certain point."

"I live by the side of a river back home in Ireland, and the river set was my favorite set. It felt like a natural thing. They had the shape of rocks, gloss on the walls, shafts of light coming down, and the little waterfall. It was a twofold scene because there was quite a bit of fight choreography that Boyd and I had to learn on the day. We finished pretty late, and [I felt like] jumping in the water to cool off! It was nice having the water around."

—Saoirse Ronan, actor

Makeup provided the look for all the injuries. To get the various cuts, Ve Neill used a three-dimensional transfer system developed by makeup artist Christien Tinsley and first used on *The Passion of the Christ* (2004). "It's sort of done the same way tattoo transfers are done, and with lots of blood," Neill explained. "The blood effect depended on what we were doing. There are different thicknesses and colors. For this film, we tended to not use bright red blood, because that would nullify our PG-13 rating. We used a little darker, toward the brown side. The blood comes in different forms—paste, thick form, a running form. I'll use a combination of a gel and a thick blood. Obviously, Andrew had a lot of say."

Many of the cuts, bruises, blisters, and bloody wounds filmed onstage had to be matched in New Mexico—a continuity nightmare for script supervisor Sullivan. It was further complicated because souls have healing sprays that make any wound vanish, so he also had to keep track of when an injury might have been healed. "The hardest [continuity] thing on this movie is probably the injuries," he said. "You can have a big cut on your arm, blood on your sleeve and stuff. The science the souls bring to this world is they

(Opposite page) Wanda and Kyle fight beside the river. (This page) A cable provides safety as Holbrook and Ronan perform a stunt in the rapids.

can heal it with a certain spray. So at this point, do we even have a wound? Is there still blood on the outfit?"

The cave set was tough for cast and crew. "Dusty," was how Max Irons summed up a stage environment that replicated the gritty reality of a windblown sandstone cavern. "The whole movie was a little bit of a challenge due to locations and moving and the whole cave set, where we did atmosphere inside the set," special effects coordinator Jack Lynch noted.

Despite the tough conditions, Max Irons credited the director and his keen eye with keeping the ensemble on track. "Andrew is amazing because he

The souls' technology allows Wanda's injuries to be healed with a spray.

Max Irons as Jared, Saoirse Ronan as Wanda, and William Hurt as Jeb perform a scene on the infirmary set.

cares about specificity, and you get more opportunities to get it right. One day we were shooting a scene and eight members of the cast were in this tiny room. We were rolling and then he went, 'Cut, cut!' And he stormed onto the set. We all assumed it was one of us! Then he found this little pile of paper napkins and took *four* of them off. Then he goes, 'Right. Good. Action!' I didn't notice that! But I'm glad he did. He sees everything."

Nick Wechsler also credited William Hurt with helping to keep spirits high. "It was a demanding physical job for all our actors, working in the caves with the bad air [onstage] and then out in the desert with the hot sun. William was just so delightful, so giving to the younger actors and to all of us. A lot of times it can get complicated when you work with established and successful actors, male or female, who have seen everything and done everything and had a lot of kudos come their way."

"You just watch and learn from people like William Hurt," Irons reflected. "William is so alive to what's in front of him. Actors talk about that but don't necessarily do it. It's the hardest thing to truly be present, to listen and respond. We're all actors, we're all egotists, and we

"You just watch and learn from people like William Hurt."

all want to get it right for ourselves and for the production. But you're still looking at yourself, and William never does that. He's always looking *out*. If someone offers something, without a moment's hesitation he bats it right back. Every take with him is different. Just getting a chance to watch a true master is priceless, really."

Ronan recalled a scene in the cave's infirmary where Hurt put on the brakes, the actors all collected themselves, and they went at it again. "It was a big scene," Ronan said, "and something wasn't feel-

Jared and Jeb face off.

ing right. We just stopped, rehearsed, and it became this fantastic scene. William is a big believer in always asking questions and trying to figure out the truth. It's easy to come in and do a scene, especially when it's a big group of people, and just say your lines and go through the action. We almost did that a few times and we stopped and said, 'Wait, what are we doing here and what is this about?'"

She summed up what the actor taught her: "William Hurt told me, 'Always remember who you are.'"

Jeb gives Jamie encouragement as Ian and Wanda look on.

CHAPTER 4
SOULS ON EARTH

e made our worlds better places; that was absolutely essential or we did not deserve them . . . We did make whatever we took better, more peaceful and beautiful. And the humans *were* brutish and ungovernable . . . Even the huge sphere of the planet had been put into jeopardy through their careless and greedy mistakes. No one could compare what had been and what was now and not admit that Earth was a better place thanks to us."[5]

In this way Wanda defends the souls, early in the novel, during some contentious inner dialogue with Melanie. To Andy Nicholson, Wanda's rationale is

> "We made our worlds better places; that was absolutely essential or we did not deserve them."
>
> — *The Host*

the stuff nightmares are made of. "In their eyes, when they took over Earth and these faulty beings, they made it passive and perfect. The horrible thing is that when they occupy the species of a world, that world doesn't develop. When you're a dominant species like we are, everything just stops. The reality is they're destroying that which makes us most specific, and flawed, as a species."

In the novel, Wanderer is introduced in her soul form as she is inserted into her new host. She's described as a "silver gleam . . . a living ribbon . . . thin, feathery attachments, nearly a thousand of them . . . like pale silver hair."[6] "The design for the souls started

with reference material from Andrew that interpreted what Stephenie envisioned while writing her novel," explained visual effects supervisor Ellen Somers. "The key is, it [the alien] is a parasite, but as it is a critically intricate element in this complex love story, we, as humans, can't be repulsed by it."

"In terms of our design, we dealt not only with form, with tentacles or filaments coming out of the body, but with light," Wechsler added. "We wanted it to look alien but not alienating."

"The great thing about the souls is they're only about three inches long," Nicholson said. "It's not some huge alien that fits into your body, but tiny things that spread out into your nervous system. The look is kind of a feathery worm, with tendrils that light up when it touches a surface. Their shape, and how these things moved, was important to work out. It was about making it otherworldly."

Early in preproduction, Nicholson argued that the souls shouldn't have a lot of high-tech stuff—the apex of their science is medical technology that's built around healing sprays. "The sprays are opaque, and so advanced you don't really see what's going on," Nicholson added. "And the souls travel through outer space in pods that are about six inches by four inches, not huge spaceships." This detail differs from the book and, according to Stephenie Meyer, was another innovation by Andrew Niccol.

The world of the souls is orderly and pristine. (Opposite page) Wanda shops at a food store, where there is no need for variety in labeling. (This page) Souls wait patiently at a healing center (above). Wanda eyes an array of healing sprays (left).

Pods, in which the souls travel through space, and podholders (left). Laser scalpels, which are used to insert souls into human bodies (right).

The "cryopods," as their ships are called, were about the size of an ostrich egg, by prop master Guillaume Delouche's reckoning. "We had to miniaturize a lot of things. We worked closely with Andrew Niccol and Andy Nicholson to create something from their vision. Everything the aliens have is reminiscent of their appearance when they're outside their human form—everything is shiny chrome and silver. So all the props had to be highly polished and laser-etched. We did all their little sprays, little laser scalpels, little phones, all those little details."

The vintage Volvo Wanda will drive looks brand-new.

Once souls are in their hosts, they wear indigenous clothing and inhabit existing dwellings, even as they reshape and perfect the world. "In the script, there are no wars and no illness," Nicholson said. "People just die of old age." Everything the souls use is kept immaculately clean, maintained, and refurbished as needed. Souls might drive a vintage car, for example, but it looks like it just rolled off the showroom floor—such as the pristine 1982 Volvo that Wanda drives to escape into the desert.

"Visually, the film becomes unique, because it is our world today but turned several degrees askew," said producer Steve Schwartz. "And that's because the aliens have taken over human bodies but are not quite sure what to do with them. They are experimenting stylistically. It takes a long time to figure out how to groove with human bodies and our possessions."

The giveaway that a soul inhabits a host is what Ve Neill calls "the halo" around the eyes, an effect created by using contact lenses (Neill herself was fitted for test photos shown to the director). A performer who didn't normally wear contacts first visited an optometrist to get lenses especially fitted for his or her eyes, and then painter and contact lens designer Cristina Patterson painted on a silver ring. "Cristina is a really talented artist who goes in with microfine brushes that are sometimes the width and length of a hair and paints the lenses to an amazing detail," explained lens technician Robert Smithson, who worked under the makeup department and was in charge of putting the contacts on actors. "I like to put the contact lenses in last. A lot of the time you're airbrushing the face with an alcohol-based makeup that can get in the eyes—that is not a healthy thing to have with a contact lens in. This was a huge show as far as contact lenses went. Just about every principal actor wears lenses, except for the humans who are the principals. We had Saoirse, Diane Kruger, other Seekers, plus background actors. On any given day we had maybe twenty-five people in lenses. I had some help making sure the actors were comfortable, but for the most part I put the lenses on the principals and also a lot of the background performers."

"The souls don't come to change a world but to experience it and perfect it. They embrace whatever technology they encounter on a world."

—Andrew Niccol

The heart of the new world is the Soul Center, built by the aliens to process humans, implant them with souls, and assimilate the new hosts. It's a practical and functional space, without warmth or frills. "We made the decision that all interiors should have an element of claustrophobia—referencing Wanda and Melanie's situation," Nicholson's production notes revealed. "Large windows that offer no view, or are merely a light source. Low ceilings. Identical doors in most rooms open onto identical corridors . . . Surfaces are practical and unembellished, concrete is concrete . . . Furniture is purely functional and as simple as possible. No

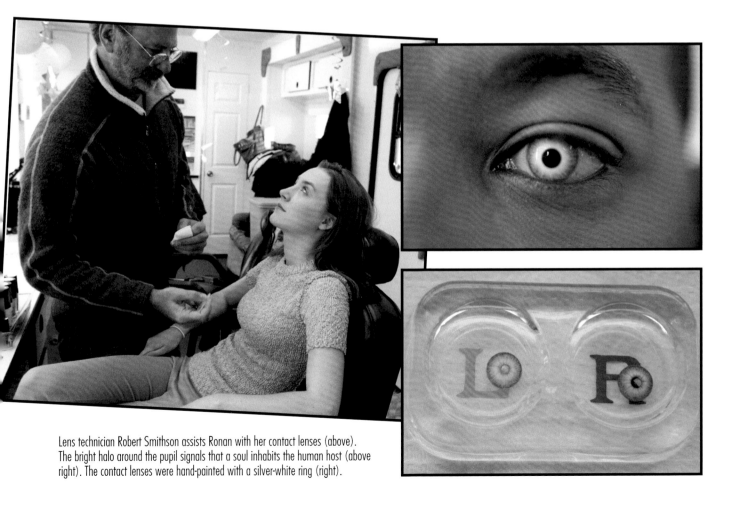

Lens technician Robert Smithson assists Ronan with her contact lenses (above). The bright halo around the pupil signals that a soul inhabits the human host (above right). The contact lenses were hand-painted with a silver-white ring (right).

electric outlets, switches or cables!"

The center included the "Mind-Reading Room" (the production designer's notes ominously describe it as a "place for reflection but also interrogation") and the "Operating Theater," an artificially lit space where souls are surgically inserted into their hosts. For the scene of Wanda being inserted into Melanie, the production designer didn't want a single operating table, as if this were a procedure just for Melanie, but a setup indicating its earliest scope. "I wanted the

Soul Center to feel like a factory. I wanted a hundred tables, something that would say how big a process it had been at one point, and wasn't anymore. They'd be doing these operations hundreds of times a day, or even hour, when they're first on a planet."

Ultimately, three tables would suffice. In a ghoulish touch, the production rented morgue tables from a coroner for Wanda's insertion. "They had drains and vents and a cantilever," Nicholson said. "They had a great design, stainless steel and very square, and

Interiors in the souls' world are practical and unembellished. Wanda's apartment (above). The Seeker questions Wanda in the "Mind-Reading Room" (right). (Opposite page) Healers prepare to insert Wanda into Melanie's body as the Seeker looks on.

looked odd and unusual."

In the novel, souls are inserted through the base of a human host's skull, at the top of the spinal column. Early in the production, it was proposed that souls enter their hosts by sliding under the eyelids. "The eyes, after all, are the windows of the soul," Niccol said. "However, Stephenie felt that due to the fragile nature of our eyes, it would be off-putting to the audience if the soul entered and exited in this manner, so we settled on the original method depicted in the novel."

A cultural aspect providing an "important glimpse into the world of the souls," in Nicholson's view, is the Megamarket. Outwardly it's a familiar-looking big-box store, only now you don't buy things—you take what you need. The products have generic labeling, and items are scanned at checkout only for restocking purposes. The Super Store Stage stood in for itself as the Megamarket the humans visit on a raid. "So much of the soul world relies on chrome as a material, and the exterior of this abandoned store already

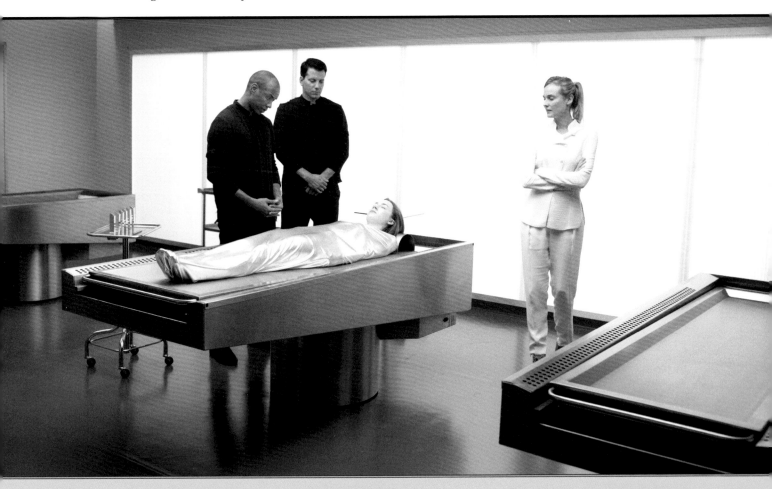

"The operation in which Wanda is inserted into Melanie isn't anything special. It's not even a supersterile room. The people who do the operation don't wear gloves. It's just an operation they've done millions of times before. The soul is the special thing; the body it's being put into is of no consequence."

—Andy Nicholson, production designer

had a polished aluminum façade," Ray Angelic said. "We just had to primp it up. It even had 'Super Store' on the outside. We just did 'Store,' and gave the non-aluminum parts of the façade a new paint job, and that was our store."

Other exterior locations reflected the director's favorite design style. "Things looked more futuristic half a century ago," Niccol said. "There is a timeless-ness, elegance, and simplicity to midcentury modern architecture and design that I thought would appeal to the souls."

The aliens' own architecture was also reflected in buildings now interspersed among the human-made structures. "Early on, it was Andrew's idea to include a

An abandoned big-box store was used as the souls' Megamarket (top and top right).
Ronan, Abel, and Irons rest between takes (above).

Wanda leaves the healing center (above). New Orleans's Garden District was used to represent a typical souls' neighborhood (right).

generic alien building in the background," Nicholson recalled. "We discussed whether it would be different types of architecture, like midcentury modern, but we came back to the idea that it needed to be instantly identifiable but also alien to our world. The best representation of that was a chrome, egg-shaped building, which also represents the pods they use to travel around in space."

However, in postproduction it was determined that a podlike building might confuse the audience. The concern was that the audience might interpret the building as a larger alien ship that had landed. So the idea never made it off the drawing board.

There were "perfect scenes," as Nicholson called them, of a typical colonized neighborhood. The production scouted Baton Rouge for examples of tidy uniformity, right down to identical mailboxes. But those neighborhoods didn't have southern oak trees to match the exterior of the Soul Center location in Baton Rouge. They found their location in New Orleans's Garden District and a neighborhood of beautifully preserved century-old homes with immaculate gardens, small lawns, and big trees. The set dressing added extra flowers and other touches, the wardrobe dressed soul folks in their best, and the location was lit to look sunny and bright. In what would be one of the serendipitous moments during filming, the camera caught lovely changes in sunlight.

"In New Orleans, you get thunderstorms that come out of nowhere, but sometimes, as you see the clouds change, it adds an idealized feeling of romance and nostalgia," Schaefer observed. "We had some of those moments when the clouds ran through and the sun came out again. It just feels like there's a bright side and happiness is about to come about."

> "In the souls' neighborhood, there could be no fences or borders, because everything is open and free. Nobody locks their doors, because they don't have to. Everything is good."
>
> —Roberto Schaefer, director of photography

Seekers at work at the Soul Center.

A soul neighborhood is perfect—no street signs, garbage cans, clutter—but the production wasn't filming in a perfect world. "Shooting exteriors in Louisiana, we couldn't take down every sign because there are signs everywhere, and garbage cans, smokestacks, cars, different things in the background," Schaefer said. "So on top of the real visual effects, like big chrome pod buildings and enhancing the silver rings in the eyes, there is a lot of invisible [digital cleanup] stuff."

"If you work with Andrew, you are *always* cleaning up the world that we shoot our movies in," visual effects supervisor Somers added. "I be-

> "The Seekers are kind of the leftover part of the attack squad that goes in at the start, when the souls are taking over a planet—they're the storm troopers, in a passive, Seeker kind of way."
>
> —Andy Nicholson

lieve it is the world he hoped he'd live in, so it is hard for me to discern what is endemic to Andrew's vision in this movie or just his view of a utopian world."

The souls are an egalitarian society, with the exception of one social unit—the Seekers, who are souls charged with the messy reality of keeping order. The novel describes them as "keepers of the peace . . . the punishers."[7] But other than the Seeker pursuing Wanda, Seekers never exceed their authority.

"I'm always thinking in terms of the character's intentions," costume designer Benach noted. "The souls and Seekers genuinely want to maintain peace on this earth. There is no hierarchy or ruling class on Earth, but there still has to be some faction that organizes things, and the Seekers are that. Seekers are assigned to new souls that are born, and I understood them to be everything from a government to a passive police force—I called them 'the municipality.' The souls are living and enjoying their peacefulness; the Seekers are sort of this municipality that keeps order."

The Seekers' fashion sense was skewed toward the art deco age of the 1930s and '40s. "My early Seeker drawings were a little out there, but Andrew wanted a modicum of 'relatability'—he didn't want this to turn into a far-fetched, über-sci-fi thing," Benach recalled. "We first went for big shoulders and a very curvy silhouette, with hats and gloves. We slowly pulled back from that, with less of a heavy hand, to a more hybrid thirties-forties silhouette."

There were six to eight white hero suits for the Seekers who accompany the main Seeker, and suits for as many as twenty to forty background Seekers. Most of the Seeker suits, based on Benach's designs, were made at a tailor shop in Los Angeles. "The Seekers wear boots, and a suit with a boot is different from a suit with a shoe, so we had to design pants to fit with that. I'd say they are elegant work suits that are functional and have a tapered leg, with jackets that aren't so tapered."

The silvery chrome theme was reflected in the Seekers' sleek cars and motorcycles. The production needed five, one of which would be crashed in the film's big chase sequence. "A lot of the car models we were considering looked aggressive, just not what the souls would be in," Nicholson said. "Lotus came up, and that was good. The Lotus cars are podlike, like the tiny alien pod craft they fly in. They're fast and agile and have a slight menace. As they were all chrome,

"The Seekers are a little different because they are looking for the last pockets of human existence. So we all look very serene, and all dress in white and drive very cool cars. My character in particular is a little different. She is a little less soft-spoken than the rest, and it makes the other Seekers wonder what is wrong with her, because in a way she's too human. She's cynical and lies, and just is not your typical Seeker."

—Diane Kruger

they looked amazing when we shot in the desert. We got great reflections of the sky and environment."

The Peace spray helps the Seekers keep order—it doesn't kill or injure, but it knocks you unconscious. An exception is used by the Seeker chasing Wanda—she wields a Glock. "The Seekers don't use guns, but the main Seeker is different from the other Seekers," Wechsler explained. Over the course of the movie, we find out more about what makes this Seeker behave so unusually.

The production had first considered the actress Eva Green for the main Seeker. The dates didn't work out, but Diane Kruger was available. "We had planned to cast an American, so we weren't sure about Eva, who is French, and we definitely weren't thinking of casting someone who was German," Wechsler said. "But Diane be-

"The Lotus cars are pod-like, like the tiny alien pod craft souls fly in."

gan to make sense. She had a determined quality that we thought would fit with the fierce determination of the Seeker. I think we picked right."

Kruger's makeup was one of the first designed by Ve Neill, the makeup artist remembered. "I used this product called Fard Creme from a French company, Le Maquillage. It's kind of a wax-based foundation. I mix it down with alcohol and put it on and it gives the skin a slick alabaster look, which is perfect, because the souls are supposed to look like perfect human beings. They've eliminated disease and injury—they get rid of everything with a simple spray. It was a simple makeup, but she looked flawless."

The Seeker was also one of Candy Neal's early concerns. "Diane was on my mind," she recalled, smiling. "The Seeker. When I read the script, I had it in my mind that Diane's hair would be off her face, twisted back like a tight French twist. Diane was happy because we both were thinking of having her hair back. And she said, 'But let's do a ponytail.' So we did, and

The Seekers drive chrome vehicles that emulate the look of their other technology.

her hair was a great color. The roots are slightly darker to add depth. And about two inches out, the ends are very pale, so it blended in very well with Ve's makeup. When you looked at her on camera in the makeup tests, everybody went, 'Wow.' Her wardrobe was all white and she was like this illuminated being. Everything just came together. Once again, it was the hair, the makeup, the wardrobe."

Lighting completed the image for the camera.

"One of the things I love about lighting is how much help you are to an actor and an actress in making them more beautiful," Paul Olinde said. "You spend a lot of time looking at actors and actresses, watching how light moves across their faces and where the shadows lie. We didn't give the Seekers a specific lighting look, but we paid close attention to Diane, our hero Seeker. She's gorgeous, she's got the crazy Seeker eyes, the beautiful blond hair—there's an air of

"Diane is that outside force that keeps coming at them. She can be really pleasantly terrifying. She has to be a soul, but there's that intensity underneath where she's just becoming so obsessed with this problem. She and Saoirse are pretty great together."

—Stephenie Meyer

Melanie jumps from a window to escape capture. Stuntperson Stacey Carino performed the fall.

perfection about all the Seekers, but especially Diane."

In the film, Melanie tries to kill herself by running down a hallway and crashing through a window to the concrete pavement below. "This was one of the big wire gags we did in New Orleans," Sam Hargrave explained. "We talked about how we wanted to shoot it, how to send her through a glass window on the fourth floor, forty feet to the ground. I ran it by Andrew and Roberto and they agreed."

The stunt was shot at a bank in New Orleans, an otherwise "ND," or nondescript, location. The action featured Stacey Carino doubling for Saoirse Ronan, while key stunt rigger Jared Eddo and riggers Thayr Harris and Adam Kirley set up a truss rig that overhung the window of the ninth floor. Carino was on a cable harness, with pic points for wires that went through tempered glass cut with a vertical slit, a two-inch gap allowing the wire to run out to the truss rig above. The special effects crew also had fastened "poppers," or controllable explosives, to the four corners of the glass. A layer of cardboard boxes was laid on the ground, covered with eight-inch mats, and overlaid with a one-inch foam pad painted to look like concrete. A C camera operator was stationed to film out of one of the upper floors, a B camera operator was on the bottom looking up (and wearing goggles to protect from breakaway glass), and the A cameraman, Jim McConkey, was cabled off so he could run with the stuntwoman without going out the window.

"We rehearsed it a bunch," Hargrave recalled. "Finally, at three-two-one-*Go*, she ran, and Jim, our A cameraman, followed. As she hit the window, special effects blew the glass by remote control, and Jim leaned out the window to follow her all the way down."

Saoirse Ronan stepped in for the aftermath, now with makeup cuts applied. "A lot of the injuries are subtle and stylized and it's Andrew's vision," Neill ex-

Ronan performs the aftermath of the fall, with injury makeup and wire pic points still attached (above). The Seekers find Melanie's broken body.

Ronan executes a daring stunt jump from a twenty-eight-foot-high balcony.

plained. "Some are almost like a dream—I don't know how else to describe it. After Saoirse has fallen through that window and she's all cut up, there is no blood. It's very stylized and odd. That was intentional. Andrew didn't want any blood and I didn't even put blood coming out of the cuts. They had red centers but they weren't bleeding. It was very dreamlike, I thought."

Saoirse Ronan did a lot of her own stunts; Hargrave pays her the ultimate compliment of being "physically capable." The most daring was a leap into water from a balcony in Baton Rouge. Although Ca-

rino did the full twenty-eight-foot jump into the water, Saoirse was shot jumping and being stopped at the twenty-foot mark. "The story point is Mel is helping Wanda/Mel escape from the Seekers," Hargrave explained. "Wanda is afraid to do it, so Mel gives her a little push." Ronan was eager to get in the harness, after first getting insurance clearance and her parents' approval.

The actress was on a gold tail wire rig, a friction system in which wires are looped through holes that slow or speed up the descent. "You always start

"We had a sequence in the bayou where Diane Kruger's Seeker and Saoirse Ronan's character have their first physical confrontation, although I wouldn't call it a fight. It was some joint locks, and Diane slams Saoirse up against a tree. Both of them were very physically capable. I was very pleased. I was very fortunate on this show that everyone I worked with was physically capable."

—Sam Hargrave

with more holes, more friction, so she goes slower," Hargrave explained. "You first test with weight bags that approximate the weight of your performer, to make sure the system will hold. When you're happy with that, you put a performer on and start slowly until you can go full speed. We put her on the line and had her jump off the balcony. She came straight from another film and into rehearsals for the acting side of this film, so I didn't get a lot of time with her. But a friend of mine, [stunt co-ordinator] Hiro Koda, and his team trained with her a lot on *Hanna*—she did some wire stuff on that. So she came to me pretty well trained. She was enthusiastic and fearless. I was stoked for her to do it, because it was going to be a great shot in the movie. And Saoirse was a rock star. She went for it! When she sits up on the edge, you look over and see there's nothing down there to catch her—and off she goes!"

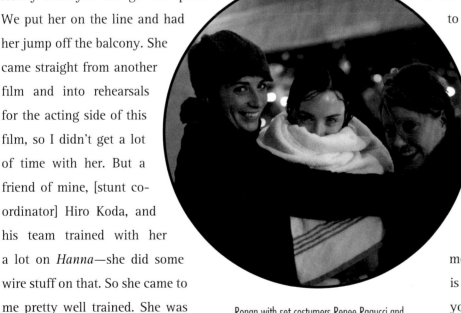

Ronan with set costumers Renee Ragucci and Gayle Anderson

"I'd never done anything like that before. It was a little bit nerve-racking," Ronan admitted. "I did a jump before, but it wasn't anything big. I worked with Sam, who is an amazing stunt fighter, and Stacey, who is a really great stunt double. I went in ahead of time just to practice and get used to that sensation of not having your feet on the ground. They had a nice small harness that fit my body well and you couldn't really see it."

There were personal incentives in doing the stunt, she added. "I wanted to do it because it was a challenge and I think it makes more of an impact when a stunt is being performed on film and you can see the actor's face. Maria [Mantia], the second AD, told me afterward that during pre-production, when they were talking about doing this stunt, the guys were all betting I wouldn't do it. Maria was the only one who thought I would—and she won the bet!"

CHAPTER 5
FIGHT FOR SURVIVAL

Wanda ventures into the desert
to find Melanie's family.

When the production arrived in Albuquerque for the last two weeks of filming, some walked a few blocks from their downtown hotel to the lively district where fabled Route 66 crosses and bought cowboy hats. "When in Rome . . ." explained a smiling Sam Sullivan, whose hat became a part of him from the Albuquerque shoot to the final days at rugged Shiprock. "I looked at the natives and I'm like, 'Wow! We're in Albuquerque and the sun's beating down. I need to find a hat that adjusts to this environment.' So this sound guy, Steve, and I went to the hat store and got cowboy hats. It's like we're doing a real Western. This is a very cool part of the script because we're done with all the lovey-dovey kissy stuff and now we're doing the arduous trekking-through-the-mountain stuff."

As filming was going on in Louisiana, location manager Rebecca Puck Stair had been busy getting yeses in New Mexico. In addition to obtaining the usual permissions (from civic leaders, police, neighborhood groups), securing locations in New Mexico means wading into complex, sometimes thorny land ownership issues that involve Indian nations or recall the era when the state was Spanish territory.

> "This is a very cool part of the script because we're done with all the lovey-dovey kissy stuff and now we're doing the arduous trekking-through-the-mountain stuff."

The sand dunes outside Albuquerque, where the production planned to film Wanda/Mel staggering through the desert and discovering Jeb's abandoned cabin, had been a land grant from the king of Spain. Known as the Atrisco Land Grant, the area had been passed down from the original Spanish settlers through their descendants and was communally owned. Any land use decision, from selling to letting a movie shoot there, had to be made by the hereditary owners—all sixty-four of them, by Stair's count. In fact they had sold the land to a New York development company, but the real estate market crashed, the sale fell through, and the land had gone into foreclosure. That left the heirs, who still felt they were the owners, a real estate developer in Arizona, and a team of lawyers in New York who were dealing with the foreclosure. "For me, the trick question was who could say yes, who could say no, as well as questions down the line: Can we grade, can we build Jeb's cabin on the land? Finally the New York lawyers signed off for us. A lot of times it's a judgment call. In this case, if anyone were going to come after us, it would be them. If *they* said yes, it was fine."

Shiprock and what the production called Horseshoe Mesa required Navajo approval. Stair notes that Ray Angelic began negotiations in October of 2011 and from there it was "four months of chipping away" to get all the permissions, including those from the Navajo film office, the equivalent of federal and local government, and the landowners. "Working

Melanie leads Wanda to Uncle Jeb's cabin.

On the way to the desert, Wanda survives a spectacular car crash (above). The Seekers investigate the scene of the crash (right). A disoriented Wanda has no choice but to try to cross the desert on foot (below right).

with the Navajo is maddening and wonderful at the same time," she reflected. "They don't have set rules like white culture. It's a lot more fluid. And just because their equivalent of the federal government says, 'Yes, you can film,' doesn't really mean you can. They can't speak for individual landowners, although [technically] there are no landowners, because the whole nation is held in trust by the U.S. government for the Navajo people. But individuals can own grazing rights to a particular piece of land. So you have to get permissions from *everybody,* and the way they negotiate is different from the mainstream. The pace can be very slow. It's Indian time. And my experience is if you make an offer and they don't like it, they just don't call you back. You have to figure out what it is about your offer that is not acceptable."

During the early location scouting trips the production team had seen New Mexico under snow, and the ensuing months still had wintry conditions. *The Lone Ranger* was already filming outside Albuquerque when *The Host* arrived, Roberto Schaefer recalled, and he knew they had been snowed out a few days. "They were just down the plain from where we were on the sand dunes. We could see the town they built from our location. Conditions were definitely weather-

dependent." But by April the weather had shifted from snowstorms to sandstorms.

"Sandstorms are kind of a normal occurrence out here," Stair explained. "We have four seasons in New Mexico: summer, fall, winter, and wind."

During the Albuquerque shoot, stunt driver Heidi Moneymaker doubled for Saoirse Ronan in a spectacular crackup of the Volvo that Wanda/Mel uses to escape the Seekers and drive into the desert. The stunt itself was a story point that came after the dramatic leap from the balcony in Baton Rouge. As they drive, Wanda and Mel get into an argument and Mel suddenly takes the wheel and jerks it violently, causing them to crash.

Jack Lynch's special effects crew built a steel roll cage for the crash car, so that the roof and sides wouldn't collapse and crush the driver. Stuntmen Chris Palermo and Jeremy Fry, who were on hand to drive in the big stunt chase sequence, added their own touches to the vital roll cage. "Special effects, Picture Cars, and stunts worked closely together to prepare the car," Hargrave noted. "Heidi was spot on—she hit her mark and did a car flip, with a cannon roll that rolled the car from wheels to wheels four times. Very spectacular! Heidi made the stunt impressive and memorable."

The ensuing scene of Wanda/Mel wandering in the desert, dying from thirst and the burning sun while searching for Jeb's cabin, was shot in the sand dunes on what was "the hardest day" up to that point, Sam

"I think there were like three sandstorms while I was there [in Albuquerque]. Almost every afternoon a window opened and the wind would start blowing the sand around. Even if it wasn't a storm, there was always very fine sand getting into lenses and computers and people's eyes and noses. It wasn't easy, but we made our days, and the changes in weather accounted for scenes with such beauty and extraordinary colors that some people will think we achieved it as a visual effect. We're going to have a hard time selling that as real, but it was!"

—Nick Wechsler

Wanda walks into the sunset (top). The crew in full sandstorm gear (middle). Stephenie Meyer and coproducer Meghan Hibbett prepare to weather another storm (above).

Sullivan said. Late that afternoon the restless wind stirred, sweeping clouds of fine, powdery sand across the plain. It built into a storm, and when the driving wind and sand hit, crew members had to hold on to production tents to keep them from blowing away. The production didn't retreat but held tight as the storm blew through the location for the next two hours.

"We thought we were getting stormed out," Schaefer said. "But then it kind of slowed down and was just picking up in the distance. We were set to shoot Saoirse wandering in the desert, heading into the sunset. And there was this incredible, eerie, beautiful golden light in the sunset because of all the sand in the air. You see her wandering into the desert and this sandstorm happening on the plains in the distance and the whole sky is turning yellow. It was pretty amazing. For me, it's one of the most beautiful visuals in the film."

After the shoot, the set for Uncle Jeb's cabin was removed. "Legally, there's always a contract with a release, so the owner of the location has a chance to sign off to say, 'Yes, I'm satisfied with the exit condition of the property,'" Stair explained. "But the film ethic is to leave things in equal or better condition than you found them. Every show I'm on we do that, and I take pride in that."

The day after the sandstorm the weather turned perfect, just in time for the scheduled chase sequence between Seekers and humans. Hargrave, who admitted that stunt driving was not his area of expertise, hired his personal all-star stunt driving team. "It was a real privilege to hire these people, because they've been doing it twice as long as I have. And it's not only what they're doing, it's how they conduct themselves on set. They're always close by, and as soon as you say, 'Hey, stunties,' they're up and ready to help with whatever you need. That's a good example for me and for up-and-coming stuntmen."

One of the stunt drivers was Melissa Stubbs. She was trained to take on every kind of assignment: martial arts fighting, high falls, burns, horseback riding, skydiving, deep-sea diving. But now, at age forty-two, she specialized in stunt driving. "My favorite things are driving cars and motorcycles—I just have a good feel for it," she said. "Early in my career, when I was about eighteen, an older stunt coordinator/director said to me, 'If you want to last long in this business, kid, become a driver. You can do that for your whole life, but you can only get hit by cars or fall down stairs or jump off

Stunt coordinator Sam Hargrave with stuntwoman Melissa Stubbs

cliffs for so long before injuries catch up with you and your body gives out.' I took that to heart and started going to racecar driving schools and learning how to race motorcycles. Being good on a motorcycle goes hand in hand with the car. It's all about feel and hand coordination and being calm in the vehicle. And I like to go fast—that's fun."

Stubbs totals up the physical injuries she's sustained across more than two decades, including concussions, a broken shoulder, broken hands and legs. She knocks wood that she's healthy and in shape. That said, she doesn't hesitate when asked the question she's heard countless times: *Why do you do it?*

"I don't know why other people wouldn't! It's just normal to me. I wanted to do stunts since I was a little kid growing up in Vancouver. I started when I was seventeen. I've never known any other way. But people look at me like I'm crazy. I think it's crazy sitting and working in a bank! I'm not crazy at all. It's not about being a daredevil. It's a calculated risk. Everything is thought out and figured out. And you work with your team. I go on gut instincts, really."

Hargrave didn't use 3-D previsualization tools to plot the sequence but went old-school: draw up your road and do a run-through with Matchbox toy cars. "Some people use cardboard; I use a yoga mat. I draw out the road, gather everybody around in a circle, place the cars, and move them."

In the chase, two Unimogs, one with Brandt and Aaron, the other driven by Jared and Kyle, are out on a foray when a Seeker patrol notices Brandt driving a little too fast. A Seeker helicopter drops down

Hargrave goes over the big chase with his stunt drivers.

to stop Brandt's vehicle, but he escapes, weaving in and out of traffic with Seeker cars, motorcycles, and helicopters in pursuit. There were seven stunt drivers: Keith Woulard doubled for Brandt, Chris Palermo and Jeremy Fry were on motorcycles, Tim Rigby was a Seeker in one of the Lotus cars, Daniel Stevens doubled for Max Irons's Jared and drove the second Unimog, Melissa Stubbs doubled for Diane Kruger on a Seeker motorcycle, and veteran Albuquerque stuntman Al Goto drove another Seeker car, while veteran pilot Fred North flew a chrome Seeker helicopter.

"We had twelve drivers in all," Hargrave explained. "In addition to our seven stunt drivers, we had five precision drivers who were moving at the beginning of the first shot. But once the helicopter dropped down in front of the Unimog, the precision drivers pulled off to the side of the road and the chase was the stunt drivers. Also, in the story there are two chrome copters, but in actuality there was one chrome picture helicopter and one camera copter. Fred North piloted the chrome helicopter for all the tricky moves, as well as the camera ship when we needed the camera really close and accurate."

"To see all these guys work, that dance they were doing out there, was brilliant."

The camera department made sure there was plenty of coverage for the chase, including a Porsche Cayenne chase car with a computerized "pursuit arm" on top with a remote head. "You can race as fast as you want to go and the camera swings everywhere," Schaefer explained. "We were simultaneously running the helicopter with an Alexa in it, plus two cameras on the ground and occasionally a Steadicam. So we had about five camera bodies. Shooting action is actually quite tedious. It's a big process of setting it all up and then waiting. You just have to be budgeted, time-wise, so you can do everything safely and properly and it doesn't look gnarly and cheap. You want to make it look believable and exciting—and it does!"

University Boulevard near Albuquerque Studios was blocked off for the sequence. "It was our playground for five days," Hargrave said, smiling. "We had three days for the part involving five Lotus cars and two motorcycles, and two days for a cat-and-mouse portion between a Unimog and a Lotus. To see all those guys work, that dance they were doing out there, was brilliant. The stakes are always elevated when you in-

The chase sequence took five days to shoot and involved motorcycles, Lotus cars, Unimogs, and a helicopter (top and bottom). Aaron shoots at his pursuers (middle).

volve motor vehicles, but that's what these guys do. They are stuntmen of the highest caliber."

One of the dangerous bits in the sequence had North drop his single-engine Eurocopter AS350 down to the freeway, bringing the Unimog driven by Woulard to a screeching stop. The location was difficult for the pilot, because there were two telephone pole wires and power lines he had to fly under. "I was maybe ten feet from the wires and three feet off the ground. It's usually not a problem to avoid wires like that, but when you have to chase a car . . ."

Peggy North, the pilot's wife, served as ground coordinator. The day of the stunt, she was stationed with the stunt coordinator, director, and first AD, and only she could communicate, via radio, with the pilot. Planning and rehearsals came down to inches and the physics for what it would take for the driver to hit his brakes—and his mark. "My wife is a pilot too and knows the way I'm flying," North explained. "The morning [of the shoot] we did rehearsals with the Uni-

Ground coordinator Peggy North and helicopter pilot Fred North

mog to make sure the driver was going to stop at the right place. Each time I allowed an extra foot, so I had a little room to play with if he exceeded his mark. Peggy has an amazing sense of observation. She could see if he might be going faster than he was supposed to, or not braking the same way. If she sees the truck is going to exceed its mark, she'll let me know and I won't go in too close. I'm there a fraction of a second ahead, because I'm making him stop. I'm super close—two or three feet away, so the skid is maybe a foot off the ground and the blade is above the cabin."

Another scene involved a truck crashing into a concrete free-way pillar. The scene was planned with a full-scale remote-controlled Unimog. The "head scratcher," according to location manager Stair, was exactly what the vehicle would crash into, as they couldn't compromise the integrity of existing structures at the location. "That's when the option of a concrete culvert came in," she said.

Down the road from the location was a construc-

"When the helicopter stopped the Unimog, *that* was exciting! Keith Woulard is a great driver, and he locked up his brakes and slid maybe ten to fifteen feet up to the helicopter as the chopper stopped in front of him—the rotor blades, from where I was standing, looked like they were inches away from the top of that truck. Fred North is an amazing pilot."

—Sam Hargrave

Jared drives one of the Unimogs that is pursued by Seekers.

tion company that had giant concrete culverts. The production bought three. On crash day, the freeway lane was closed and a crane lifted the concrete culverts into place. The special effects crew bolted them together, forming a barrier thirty feet long by ten feet deep and weighing 140,000 pounds, according to special effects coordinator Jack Lynch. The art department then dressed the barrier to look like part of the freeway.

Lynch and his team had developed and tested their RC Unimog in Baton Rouge and tested it again at the Albuquerque location. "Nowadays, because of technology, people are doing more and more remote-control gags," Lynch noted. "In the old days, signals were the same—everybody had radios and phones that could interrupt [a radio-controlled signal]. But now we have special high-tech remote-control stuff— 'spread spectrums' is what they're called. The signals going between receiver and transmitter can't get

crossed or jammed. We didn't want a car going amuck down the middle of the median at sixty miles an hour. We utilized the vehicle as it was; we just put a gear right up to the steering wheel and one of the toggles could control the steering, left or right. We put in linear actuators that allowed us to remote-control the brake and gas pedal. We also built in a fail-safe kill switch so we could cut the engine, and that would automatically apply the brake. As special effects guys, we'll usually put explosions and stuff in there [for a crash]. But the director didn't want explosions, fireballs, or anything. He just wanted it to be about the guys crashing into the wall. We had an engineer come and spec everything and make sure we were doing it right, because the location was at the edge of a bridge and we didn't want to ruin anything."

The Unimog was dressed with life-sized dummies and the stunt was on. "We did the lead-ups to

Niccol directs a stunt sequence in which a Lotus crashes into a Unimog.

the crash with our stunt driver Keith," Hargrave explained. "Then we kind of stood aside and watched the special effects guys do their thing."

Jack Lynch estimated their full-scale Unimog at around 7,000 pounds, but when it hit at top speed, it moved all 140,000 pounds of concrete barrier back four inches. "The impact was pretty great," Lynch said, with understatement.

After the crash, Jared's Unimog is pursued in the cat-and-mouse portion of the sequence. As the Seeker closes in, Jared suddenly slams on the brakes, causing the Seeker's car to smash into the rear of his four-wheeler. "You're driving a luxury sports car and get to crash into the rear end of a military vehicle—that's a dream day for a stunt guy," Hargrave observed. "Daniel

Stevens drove the Unimog, while Keith Woulard and Chris Palermo crashed the Lotus on different takes."

In the first try, the Lotus didn't hit the Unimog hard enough. In take two, the Lotus came in "hot" and smashed up good—but it wasn't the sideways approach Niccol wanted. The crew broke for lunch, and special effects and the picture car department went to work. "The front end was smashed up into the windshield. That car looked *totaled*," Hargrave recalled. "During lunch Adam Pinkstaff and Gino [Hart], the guys of Transpo and Picture Cars, and Jason [Babin] from spe-

Ian leads Wanda on a rare walk outside.

cial effects flattened the front and fixed it up with silver paint and tape. It was unbelievable. Not only was it drivable, but after lunch we got two more takes out of it! The third take we got the slide up. It still wasn't quite deep enough, but it was a good little rehearsal. The fourth take came in really hot, got it nice and sideways, and smashed into the Unimog, and that was the end of the day for the Lotus. Normally it would be one take, but we got four takes at it, a lot of footage to chop around and make an exciting crash. That was the last of the real car stuff."

After completing its Albuquerque shoot, the production moved on to its base in Farmington for the final four days of filming, which began on Tuesday, April 24. Many left Albuquerque on Monday, making the four-hour drive to the state's northwest corner in production vans. But the director, production designer, and director of photography had

"When we were driving up to Shiprock for the first time, I was just in awe of the place."

gone ahead on Friday and made one final scout. In addition to Shiprock, they went out to Horseshoe Mesa. The latter location actually comprised a grouping of four mesas, known to the locals and roughly translated from the Navajo language as Skinny Top, Blue Hill (or White Hill), Flat Top, and Palmer Mesa, the latter the actual spot they planned to film. During that final scout, the director decided to film the main cave exterior at Shiprock.

"When I met up with them on Sunday night, they said, 'We're flip-flopping everything,'" Ray Angelic recalled. "Our four days were originally going to be one day at Shiprock and three days at what we called Horseshoe Mesa. But they had scouted it and said it made more sense to do three days at Shiprock, that it was much more iconic and amazing-looking. So a couple days before we were supposed to shoot, they reconceived where the cave

"Shiprock was not the way I envisioned the caves in the novel, but it's perfect for the story we're telling now. From overhead you can see this ridge of rock that looks almost like a spine coming up to a skull, which is amazing. I spent so much of the book talking about that part in the back of your neck where the aliens invade you, and it looks like that from the air! It couldn't have been better if we had built it ourselves."

—Stephenie Meyer

would be and how we'd divide up the work between the two locations."

"The funny thing is we didn't choose Shiprock as the main cave exterior until the last week when we were shooting there," Roberto Schaefer added. "We thought the mesa was going to be the main cave area. But there were no fissures on top of the mesa. It was solid ground. We had to believe sunlight could get through and filter down into the caves and rooms and not be visible from outside. Andrew felt he could get a lot more done at Shiprock, this incredible volcanic formation that is supposed to be twenty-seven million years old. It's mysterious on top, so high up that unless you're in a helicopter you can't look down on it. It was highly believable that there could be lots of nooks, crannies, and hidden spaces where sunlight could get in, but you wouldn't know it from the outside."

Shiprock was a dramatic change from Picacho Peak, a park in Arizona where the cave of the novel is set. "I live in Arizona, so what I pictured in the book was Picacho Peak, the whole bit," said coproducer Meghan Hibbett. "When we were driving up to Shiprock for the first time, I was just in awe of the place. I've had the opportunity to travel a lot, but I've never seen anything like it. It's amazing. And the feeling you get being here is kind of surreal, almost eerie."

To the Navajo, Shiprock is sacred ground. In geologic terms it's a plug. "Shiprock is a granite plug of an ancient volcano that came up out of the earth millions of years ago," Rebecca Puck Stair explained. "There was a weak spot in the crust, and under pressure this magma squirted up like crème brûlée through its crust. Then it hardened and all the soft material around it eroded away and you're left with the plug. I like to look at Shiprock in the morning. If you kind of look at it the right way and use your imagination, you can almost feel it's still this liquid magma coming up."

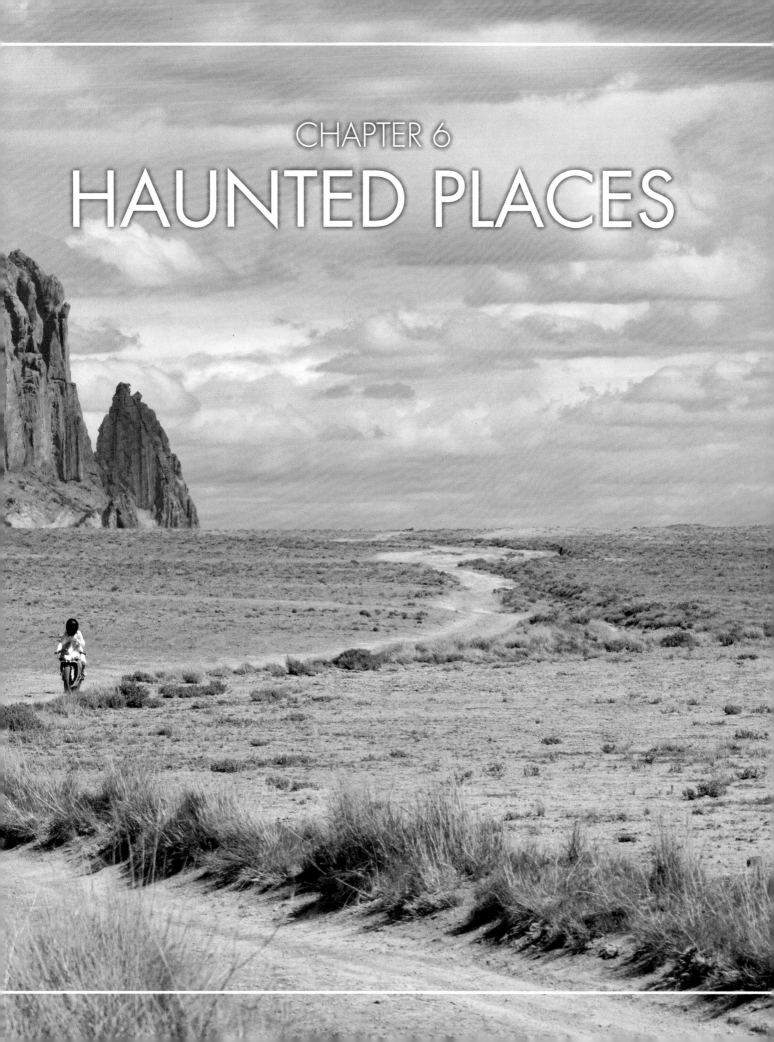

CHAPTER 6
HAUNTED PLACES

t's Tuesday, the first day of the last week of filming, and the morning schedule includes a blindfolded Saoirse Ronan, complete with halo-effect eyes, being led over a ridge by a gun-toting William Hurt, along with Boyd Holbrook, Jake Abel, Mustafa Harris, Lee Hardee, and Frances Fisher. Between takes, Fisher pulls out an umbrella to protect her from the sun as she and the others head for an open tent. Crew members slather on sunblock and cover their noses and mouths with kerchiefs, highway-robber style, to keep from breathing wind-blown dust. A team of medics is on hand to deal with any emergency and to make sure people stay hydrated; it's a regular job for the craft services department to deliver pallets of bottled water from the production's base camp. It's so dry that no one sweats. The landscape to the distant cloud-shrouded mountains is broken up with ridges, dips, gullies, valleys, and wind-carved formations. And above all looms the volcanic pinnacle of Shiprock.

Wind and dust were of concern to all departments. "We have to be prepared, of course, with different tools to adjust to the environment," key grip Bubba Sheffield noted. "We have to cover up cameras and secure them, we have to have sand screens and wind screens, or keep the camera from shaking from the wind. Other items we tie down to whatever we find available so they don't blow around."

"On location it's a long day and never very glamorous."

Lens tech Robert Smithson had to be vigilant to see that dust didn't get into the eyes of his actors. "Out here in the desert, I'm kind of the nagging mother, especially to Saoirse. I make sure the actors drink lots of water, that their eyes are hydrated with eyedrops, that they stay out of the sun until they have to be in front of the camera. And in dusty conditions, safety glasses need to be worn. It's easy to have a piece of grit or sand go into your eye, where it can make its way under the contact lens and just your normal eye movement can scratch the cornea. My job is about keeping the actors safe and helping the director and director of photography get the look required to make the film pop."

Tuesday's shooting schedule included driving shots of the Unimog leaving on a foray to the Megamarket. As the morning went on, Stephenie Meyer talked about the location. "Outdoor shooting is always the most beautiful—you get the best stuff. But each one has its own challenges, just getting to it and dealing with the terrain. I like the comfort of a soundstage. I mean, on location it's a long day and never very glamorous." She chuckled. "It's so funny. People think we're walking around in stilettos. I try to explain, 'No! We're eating dirt all day and we're in our grubby clothes and it's dirty and gross.' But then you have those moments, like driving up today to Shiprock. The landscape here is just the most amazing thing. And you think about it in terms of the story and imagine it all fitting together and it is a surreal and crazy feeling."

"Shiprock looks unreal from base camp and where the working

Letting off some steam while on location (left to right): Ronan, Hibbett, coproducer Elizabeth Bradford, Meyer, Irons

trucks are," said Mustafa Harris as he waited for the scene where he would help bring in the captured Wanderer. "I almost wish I'd seen this before we shot the interior work, just because having this in your mind is a potential tool you can use for performing. I'm seriously in awe. I think when audiences see it, they're not going to believe this place actually exists. They'll think it's computer-generated. But I've seen it!"

Base camp was the production's command center and gathering point. Here were trailers for production offices and actors, makeup, hair, wardrobe, and other departments, "honeywagons" (as restroom facilities are called), and a huge tent stretched over the desert floor where craft services provided breakfast and lunch. It was only a few miles from the slopes of Shiprock, but a slow, bumpy thirty-minute drive down a rocky and eroded dirt road. Production vans, which regularly made the round trip, took all cast and crew to base camp for lunchtime. The camp included a

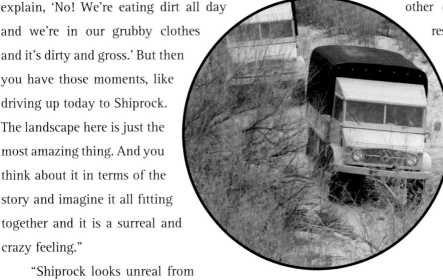

Unimogs leave the humans' stronghold.

The production prepares to shoot a scene involving the Seekers, with the majestic Shiprock peak in the background (above). Ronan and Abel between takes (left).

plain house where a Navajo family could be seen sitting on the front porch watching the circus. "Basically, our base camp is set up in their front yard," Rebecca Puck Stair explained. "I'm learning that this family has been on this land for over two hundred years. The Navajo are very nomadic, and this is their summer home. This is the stuff you learn out here."

During a crowded lunchtime in the tent, Stair sat at one of the long folding tables with Lloyd Smith and other liaisons to the Navajo nation. It turned out that the production needed another approval to shoot at Horseshoe Mesa on Friday, the last scheduled day of filming. What had seemed all set was suddenly up in the air. "I had thought we had Friday's location settled and I was going to have an easy afternoon," Stair said with a stoic smile.

The location meeting with the Navajo representatives broke up, the lunch rush was over, and the tent

"Locations straddle the world between reality and movieland. I like to think of my job as building the sandbox for the kids to play in. Once the boundaries are set up, I kind of leave them alone. I just make sure they don't leave the box. Here are your parameters, here's what you can do—now, go play. And then I worry about tomorrow's sandbox."

—Rebecca Puck Stair, location manager, New Mexico

was practically empty. "One of the things I love about locations is how you can walk into a place like this that looks relatively empty, and as you start asking questions, it reveals its story to you," Stair reflected as she sat at one of the vacated tables. "Who has been here when, why, how long, who lives here now? We were up in another location yesterday and someone happened to look down and right there was some ancient Indian pottery! Tomorrow, when we're back there, I'll point it out to our liaison, and that's their decision [what to do with it].

"Lloyd sidled up to me and said, 'You know, if you're here late at night, the west side of Shiprock *glows*. I don't know if it's the uranium or the skinwalkers, but it glows.' During part of that conversation, he was warning me about the skinwalkers. He said, 'Be careful when you're out here, because the evil is here. There are six places on the Navajo reservation where skinwalkers meet, and we're really close to one of them. So don't go that way.' I know very little about skinwalkers, except I wish white culture had a parallel. I take skinwalkers as a metaphor for the underbelly of culture, the bad and harmful element of us personified. I take it as a warning to watch out for the evils that lurk among and within us all." And there was something else, Stair thought. This movie, about invaders taking over a world, had happened. *This* was one of the conquered places . . .

"I like being in the desert. It's like costume, being in the place that you're actually supposed to be in—it informs everything about the way your character moves and thinks and exists. And it's totally different from England, you know—you've got cougars here and bears and rattlesnakes. We've got sheep and cows and ducks. So for me it's very exciting to be here."

—Max Irons

Holbrook and Irons take a break.

"I live in country like this. I mean, certainly not this dramatic, but this arid. And I love it 'cause it's in my blood and it's in my mother's blood. You know, in the desert you can remember your name. So this is a sacred place, and I think anybody who doesn't know that when they look at it must be completely insane."

—William Hurt

As the first day's shooting continued into the afternoon, the wind began acting up. Helicopter pilot Fred North was shooting aerial scenes at the rock wall spine of Shiprock, and heat and wind were a problem as he went up with his camera operator and the director. The wind was blowing off the wall, creating a vortex that could push his copter down, even make the engine quit, if he got caught in it. He stayed in the safe zone, thanks to years of experience and thousands of hours of flying time.

"It's a narrow window you play with," North said later. "I have to be on top of my game, no room for error. To have lift you need cool air, but if it's a really hot day the air expands so the blade has nothing to fly on—the machine gets lazy. So you have to be in the right place, depending on the shape of the rock, to avoid the wind that can put you down. You have to feel the machine, and nothing in the book is going to tell you if you can do it or not do it. It's experience. Originally the director wanted me to hover fifty feet off the ground. It was the first time for me to work with him and I was pushing the helicopter a little bit to show him what we can do. I like to do action stuff that's dynamic, with energy. I told him, 'Let me show you what we can do and you make the decision.' And I showed him. He was really cool—he liked the stuff."

As the helicopter flew overhead, Roberto Schaefer's cameras got long views of Seeker stunt doubles on motorcycles riding down the dusty road on one side of the wall. Andy Nicholson, dressed in a black T-shirt, stood in the adjacent field, noting the long shadows and changing light. "I think the first time we came to Shiprock we were worried it was too iconic and theatrical, that it would be too obvious as the cave. But now that we shot all the cave interiors and sort of got that out of our system, it was *not* too much. This place is more cinematic, but it's not been seen to death."

One of the Navajo working on the film was Willis Lee, a member of the liaison group who was mainly looking after the land during filming. *The Host* was his first movie work, a new experience from his regular job. Although the Four Corners region promotes recreation and tourist diversions, the local economy is about Big Energy—oil, coal mines, power plants. Lee worked in a coal mine in the nearby town of Waterflow.

Wednesday morning at base camp, Lee recalled that some in the production had already found arrowheads and pottery up in the long rock wall. He mentioned rumors of UFOs and the fires of secret skinwalker ceremonies that were said to burn during long nights at Shiprock. "Yesterday one of the producers was climbing along the rock wall and he found a sheepskin on the floor that had rocks surrounding it in a weird pattern. In our tradition, a lot of people do certain ceremonials out here in the rock area. And sometimes there'll be some bad practices as well, witchcraft and skinwalkers and stuff like that. I'm not too sure what it was, but I suggested to him not to be around that area or bother it. It could be a bad omen, or a taboo.

"There were a lot of traditional stories I heard growing up around here. A lot of the elders consider this place sacred, and at the same time it's a landmark, a monument. The mythology of Shiprock is that it's supposed to be a large bird, almost vulturelike, that used to feed on some of the Indians in this area. And somehow it settled right here and turned to stone and that's how the Shiprock rock came to be." One could make out a head, like a prehistoric flying reptile, and the peaks of the mountain had the shape of gigantic

> "This place is more cinematic, but it's not been seen to death."

Diane Kruger as the Seeker

folded wings. The wall of rock trailing from it, Lee explained, was either the creature's tail or the eruption of earth when it crashed and turned to stone.

Shiprock was more than another movie location, although its primordial grandeur was cinematic. It was a sacred mountain, an area where families had lived for generations, a land exploited for its natural resources, a state of mind steeped in the mystery and mysticism of an ancient culture.

"This is amazing. I love it here," Saoirse Ronan said during a break. "I've shot in the desert twice, but only in the Sahara, which is beautiful, but it's either sand dunes or rocky terrain. You don't really get anything like Shiprock. And also the Native American culture, it's nice to be around that. I'd never really been introduced to it before. The Navajo were very welcom-

"I'm from the Shiprock area, Navajo reservation. I was born here in Shiprock and raised here. I love it out here. A lot of people are related, clan-wise. It's a system that originates all the way back with our grandfather's grandfathers. We could be relatives from long ago through marriages or certain bloodlines. I served my time in the army as well. I went to Iraq for a four-year tour. I got out of the desert here but ended up going to a different desert in Iraq. It was quite an experience."

—**Willis Lee**, Navajo liaison

ing. They gave me a gift of a necklace they had made for me because they heard that I was here and they wanted to welcome me onto their land, and they gave me an arrowhead too. They're just lovely, lovely people and very friendly and came over to get their photos taken. And I was hearing about the skinwalkers. And there was this Navajo guy as well who believes there are Sasquatch that live over in those mountains. All these legends are wonderful—we have them at home in Ireland. I think there's something magical about our culture, and theirs as well. It's nice to be around that and to have that in common, the different stories and myths, magical creatures and legendary figures."

No one, it seemed, enjoyed the location more than William Hurt. "I think he was just basking in Shiprock. He totally loved the place," Roberto Schaefer recalled. "Maybe it was the history, the native spirit, the magnificence of the outdoors. I know one day he walked from Shiprock back to base camp; he didn't want to take a van ride. It's clear and flat, so you won't get lost, but that's like a three-and-a-half-mile walk through the desert!"

From that first day at Shiprock, Hurt was in his element, alert to even a lizard slithering through the shade of the open tent at the location. "That's a nice one," he said, grinning. Seemingly out of habit, he defensively acknowledged that he can be "prickly," a small word for an actor with his share of controversy and bad press in the fishbowl of Hollywood stardom—an actor to whom the word "difficult" was often applied, along with phrases like "leading man of the eighties" (he won his Best Actor Oscar for the 1985 film *Kiss of the Spider Woman*). Hurt shrugged it all off, went straight for the joy. He smiled as he

Ronan in full sunburn makeup, with her father, Paul Ronan (top). Executive producer Ray Angelic and Ronan (bottom).

mentioned recently performing in a Pinter play with his son.

Hurt looks askance at Hollywood and its celebrity machine, even though he's done a few popcorn pictures (he was General Ross in *The Incredible Hulk* [2008]). But he knows his Hollywood history, and referred to the golden age that was made up of war veterans and wanderers, laborers and immigrants, the era when many early screen actors honed their craft on the stages of the Yiddish theater or in vaudeville. "Sure, I would have liked to have worked then," he said wistfully. "People brought life experience to their

Irons and Abel take a break on set.

roles. In today's celebrity culture, stars are malleable and easily manipulated." He bristled at the memory of a review that mentioned his outshining fellow actors in a movie scene. "It's *not* about that, it's about the ensemble. I'm not playing Jeb. It's about the world!" He gazed up at the peak of Shiprock. "*This* is a postcard, but to the aboriginal people, it was part of who they were—they were *grounded*. They always knew where they were."

But don't tell Hurt he's a storyteller. "A storyteller is someone who is reading a book to kids. It's not about storytelling, it's *I am the story!* That camera is more than steel and glass—it's a paintbrush." *Know*

who you are. Know where you are.

Nowadays Hurt likes to write epitaphs. "We all die alone," he said with a conspiratorial whisper. But that knowledge can free you to make brave choices. There's wonder in that journey, and Hurt noted the teachers who had guided him. He mentioned his mother and, most recently, Andrew Niccol. He affectionately called the director "crazy," spoke of Niccol's screenplay, which first drew him in, and added that *The Host* might be his favorite movie experience.

By Wednesday the story time line had jumped from the sunburned Wanda being led to the cave to "several weeks" ahead, Sam Sullivan explained. "We

"I'm having one of the best times of my life with Andrew. I really think he's special. He's hands-on, he never sits all day long. And he never meddles in things he doesn't understand, which, for an intelligent, knowledgeable person is extraordinary."

—William Hurt

shot the stuff where she had sunburn and blisters and was dehydrated and near death. Now she's rested for several weeks, the blisters are gone, the sunburn has kicked off, and she's fresh and lovely again."

That afternoon, while a scene was being shot on a cliff of the spine, Ve Neill and Candy Neal were below, sitting in chairs under an open tent. It was windy and dusty, but they were out of the sun. "How are you enjoying your vacation, ladies?" a crew person asked, and they laughed. "Cocktails will be right out!"

Neill talked about Saoirse

Kruger has her makeup refreshed.

Ronan's sunburn makeup from the previous day. "That was a quickie. The director said, 'Paint her pink because it's a faraway shot.' I painted it on her so it looked like her blisters were on. When I usually do that kind of makeup, I start out with an ager, something I developed on *Pirates* [*of the Caribbean: At World's End*], just to give a rugged, crispy, and dried look to the skin. On top of that I put a little bit of liquid latex. As it starts to dry, I peel it up, pop the dried latex open so it looks like her sunburn is starting to peel. I did similar things on her lips and cracked them and put little blood marks in between where they cracked. She gradually gets more and more burned by the sun, to where she's almost dead when they find her in the desert. Poor thing, she's constantly getting injured in this movie! She gets hit, cuts, and sunburns. You name it, it happens in this movie.

"When you're in the elements you have to keep reapplying. Sometimes you just don't want to mess with it, so you kind of fluff around a little bit. Like today, I went to go touch Diane up and she was just

packed with this fine powder over her entire face. The minute I touched it and tried to repair one little spot, I wound up having to redo her whole forehead. I would have had to take everything off and start over. I said, 'I'm just going to leave everything as it is. You just look like you have a little bit of a tan right now, and that's fine.' And she was fine with that."

During the week, Melissa Stubbs was stunt doubling for Diane Kruger on the motorcycle and in the Lotus. One of her car stunts was a camera drive-by on the nearby highway. She hadn't driven the car before but realized it had been "abused" from earlier stunt work. "I jumped in and the alignment was off. I was getting it up to one-twenty on the straightaway, one hundred twelve to one hundred fifteen miles an hour past the camera crew. It felt weird and was floating all over the road. But I knew I could handle it."

Wanda's severely sunburned look was created using a multistep application process.

Jeb takes aim.

By late afternoon the production crew was fighting the light, trying to squeeze shots in before dusk ended their day. They were focused on a trail along the rock wall that dipped down into a minicanyon and looked out on the plain. William Hurt was braced against the slope, aiming Jeb's badge of authority. Someone shouted, "Fire in the hole!" Blanked guns were fired and twin bursts of gunfire echoed off the rock walls.

"What's fascinating about film," Sam Hargrave reflected, "is when you see this cut together you're not going to know they framed the camera tight enough so you don't see the stunt mats, so you can do a dramatic fall, come back to the smoking gun, and come back and start on the body on the ground. [One actress] was taking big falls on our eight-inch crash mats, which is no guarantee that you still won't hurt yourself. But she was game."

That Wednesday there was the sense of the production winding down. Frances Fisher shot her last scene that day and William Hurt, an old friend, saw her off at base camp. The next day Maggie's wig was on its way back to Los Angeles and Natascha's stockroom. "Saoirse has her extensions and it's pretty straightforward," Candy Neal summed up. "Friday is supposed to be the last day of shooting, so everybody is set. There are no more hairstyles."

On Thursday morning coproducer Meghan Hibbett was at base camp with strange tales of the previous day. "There was a going-to-kill-us rattlesnake over by craft services, and they chopped its head off with a shovel. I was present, but I didn't participate in its demise. And we found out later from one of our location guides that it's a bad omen to kill a rattlesnake and it was probably a skinwalker and we're all going to die in our sleep!" She laughed. "I believe there are skinwalkers. I feel a creepy vibe off Shiprock. I was afraid to go to sleep last night, but maybe I'm a little naive. This is what making a movie is like! It's surreal. You come out to these haunted

"You come out to these haunted places and people tell you you're going to be killed in your sleep."

places and people tell you you're going to be killed in your sleep. But I'm lucky to be able to come and work with my best friend. It might sound cheesy, but you come and you make a family. Tomorrow is our last day, and some of the people we won't ever see again."

Throughout the morning there was a serene stillness around Shiprock, with sunlight sifting down and bringing out colors in the rocky landscape. Clouds were smeared like feathery brushstrokes, and distant patches of bluish shadows in the sky showed "dry lightning," where rain evaporates before it hits the ground. One of the sequences to be shot was for Ronan's character, and costume designer Erin Benach provided a "rocker chick outfit" for the occasion. "We dressed her in this free, feminine outfit. This is a pop costume, as I call it. It pops out the character in the scene."

Max Irons as Jared

"Today I said to Ve that if they did do a sequel, it will be kind of great for me," Ronan said between takes. "Usually the problem when you do sequels is that you're always playing the same character, but I'd actually get to play a different character for the second film.

"You know, at the start of the week I was ready to go home. But it's the next-to-last day now, and usually around this time you realize, 'Oh, this is actually ending tomorrow.' And you're not going to be with the same people every day. There's a lot of people I've become close to on this and I'm going to miss not being with them every day. You'll bump into them at some stage, but you're never, ever going to have this group of people around you again, not exactly. There's a dynamic that you get used to on set, the different energies. I'll miss it. I'll be sad tomorrow. A happy thought? I'm going back to Ireland. I got my Navajo jewelry. Don't tell Ve and Candy, but I got them something nice from this place in Santa Fe."

After lunch, Max Irons leaned against a trailer, facing the desert. This was his last day, but he wasn't heading directly home to England. In the middle of the night he was to be taken to Albuquerque to catch an early morning flight to L.A. and another movie audition—one of those proverbial kill-for roles. A big grin spread across his face as he talked about learning to drive on the production and getting a Louisiana driver's license (an auto not being so useful back in traffic-clogged London). "I love it! It's brilliant. I've never felt so free and independent

"You look way ahead, take a deep breath, and feel it through. It's all about feel. I had to rip along the road in the Lotus and then I had to pretty much do off-road driving on a motorcycle built for road racing. You just have to adapt to every situation."

—Melissa Stubbs, stunt double

and grown up. We've been driving these Unimogs up and down hills, screeching around corners. It's nice when you do movies where you learn skills."

The wind was starting to stir as he reflected on his growing immersion in "the dark arts," otherwise known as movie acting. "In theater acting you do it night after night and you can get into finer detail as you go on. But with film, what you do on that day is written in history. The stops and starts, the fragmentation, is weird. On a movie production, you have to know *everything* about where you've been and where you're going, particularly when a preceding scene might have been shot months before. I think we shot one of the final scenes the first day, so you have to be aware that any decision you make at the beginning is going to affect you at the end. You've got to stay true to what you did the first day, you've got to have it all figured

"Acting is still a challenge to me, but one I hope gets clearer as time goes on."

out. It's still a challenge to me, but one I hope gets clearer as time goes on."

He reflected on what would stick with him about making *The Host*. "I'd say being at Shiprock. I've never been to a place like this in my life. It's like being on another planet. And William Hurt is going to stick with me. It's odd—it's always the little things. It's the truck rides you have to the set and back with the other members of the cast, the conversations, the jokes. They're the things that stick with you."

After lunch, William Hurt was walking around the base camp trailers saying good-bye to various production people. He mentioned visiting the home of the Navajo family at base camp and learning the ancient myths of Shiprock. And then, with hugs and handshakes and good-byes, he was in his car and gone.

When the production broke for lunch, the crew

found themselves in a holding pattern—the problem that had put the Horseshoe Mesa location in limbo had now caused a shutdown at Shiprock. The Navajo nation's fish and wildlife division had to certify that the production was not working in an endangered species area or an archaeologically sensitive site. There were rumors that it would be hours before the production would get to film—provided, of course, that permission was granted.

But then the wind picked up, snapping the flaps of the base camp tent and stirring clouds of sand and dust. The horizon began to darken with windblown waves of sand moving in as fast as a speeding car. Roberto Schaefer was on the slope of Shiprock when he and the crew saw it approaching. The assistant directors and production assistants, gaffers, and riggers helped break down the camera equipment and get it to safety.

"Absolutely, the camera equipment was in danger," Schaefer recalled. "Besides the danger of the glass getting sandblasted, the sand is really fine, and with winds blowing forty-five to sixty miles an hour, it gets into *everything*. The cameras are all electronic, so sand can mess up circuit boards and make false contacts or just stop working. We used a lot of plastic bags [to cover equipment] and had to take everything and put it in the trucks at base camp. It was so fierce! The wind was howling and the parked trucks were all bouncing left and right and their roofs were heaving up and down. It really felt as if some of the big trucks, the forty-footers, were going to blow over. I understand the catering tent blew away that day—it went flying across a field and they had to bring in a new one."

When the full force of the sandstorm hit, Shiprock became invisible and the entire area became lost in a gritty brownout.

"I turned eighteen [on this shoot] and it's a big birthday, especially at home in Ireland, 'cause you're basically an adult. Legally you're an adult, but I don't think I act like an adult, clearly. And Ve Neill, who is the best makeup artist in the world, decorated my trailer for me, and she decorated the hair and makeup truck for me. And they got cake and they hired a band. And it was wonderful. You know, when the whole crew do something collectively that's separate from actually making the film, it's really very touching."

—Saoirse Ronan

CHAPTER 7

"THE FIRE OF THIS MOVIE WORLD"

The sandstorms that created difficult conditions also brought epic sunsets.

On Friday morning the production was nowhere near Horseshoe Mesa but was filming in a field a few miles from Shiprock. It was windy, but nothing like the previous day's winds, which reportedly had reached speeds of sixty miles an hour. The air was clear, and every crack, crevice, and fissure of Shiprock was in stark relief against the blue sky.

Stunt coordinator Sam Hargrave was at the shooting site wearing his wide-brimmed hat, along with dark glasses and a blue neckerchief to cover up if things got dusty. "Yesterday the gusts were blowing down tents and it got to where you couldn't even see Shiprock," he said. "I was at base camp. It only took about ten to fifteen minutes for the dust storm to roll in. Oh, man, it was crazy. I was prepared because I had goggles and the mask, but I'd

Niccol with director of photography Roberto Schaefer (left) and camera operator Jim McConkey (right)

never seen anything like it. I've shot in New Mexico before, and seen dust storms, but not like that. Even the locals said that it was abnormally strong. We waited to see if it would blow over, but it showed no signs of stopping. We were told it was supposed to get worse so we should leave *now*. It was a little windy on the highways, but not enough to blow over a truck or car.

This morning the guys at the honeywagons were cleaning everything out. Even if a door was closed, there'd be sand inside. The sand is so fine, and the wind was so strong, it gets in through any little crack."

"The sandstorms were something I'd never encountered before," Andrew Niccol recalled after filming wrapped. "Fortunately, they would often end as quickly as they began, apart from the storm that shut us down for half a day. There was a silver lining. The same winds that brought the sand also brought spectacular cloudscapes and epic sunsets."

Location manager Rebecca Puck Stair had been out in the storm with the Navajo naturalists, reviewing the shooting locations at Shiprock and the mesa. It took the whole afternoon and they did what they could under the storm conditions, she said. The sites were okayed for filming, and the production made up its lost half-day at Horseshoe Mesa on Saturday.

There was talk that the sandstorm had been a skinwalker spell, but most locals said it was simply the power of the mountain. "'It's the rock,' someone said—it was the dark magic of Shiprock," Stair recalled. "In a sense, the windstorm saved the day, because they needed to survey both sites and the production would have had to shut down anyway. And maybe Shiprock was angry [for the killing of the rattlesnake the day before]. But to the Navajo, there is the dark side and the positive side. You need the day and the sun, and you also need the night and the moon. You need both. They go together."

In the field where the production was shooting, four reflective chrome Lotus cars were lined up on a dirt road, along with Seekers in their white suits. Gaffer Paul Olinde was scanning the sky, the only one of the crew in white shirt and tie. "I have a ritual," he said with a grin. "I always wear a tie every Friday. Yes, it's

Niccol directs Abel and Ronan in a scene at Horseshoe Mesa.

white shirt and tie out here in the desert." He smiled stoically at the question of the morning: *How is your equipment after the storm?* "The equipment is *trashed*. This morning everyone was out with the cans of air, spraying dust out of every nook and cranny and piece of gear. There is dust in everything. It operates, but we spent a lot of time cleaning the equipment, especially camera gear, which is a lot more sensitive. The electronics can take a beating from the dust."

Olinde looked up into the sky at the layers of bright clouds moving with the wind. "*There's* that cloud I have to pay attention to," he noted, vigilantly keeping an eye on one drifting cloud. "I'm concerned when we have a cloudy day. For continuity's sake, I'll stand by and watch when clouds roll in. If the

"We were lucky to have some of the best location people I've ever worked with on a movie. They deserve all the credit for getting permission to shoot [in Shiprock]. Of course, we tried to be extremely respectful. We never set foot on Shiprock Peak itself, and in every spot where we filmed, we cleaned the location of litter, leaving it better than we found it. We also worked with a number of Native Americans in the cast and crew."

—Andrew Niccol

crew is getting ready to roll and a cloud will blow a take, I'll warn the assistant directors not to roll. But when you're in the desert like this, it's gorgeous. You don't do a thing. When you're in the desert and the sun is shining, you let the sun be the sun. But continuity is very tough in this environment, very tough. We've had cloudy days and windy days. You get dust storms rolling in and suddenly your background doesn't look the same. The lighting can change."

They were ready to roll and Diane Kruger stepped in front of a silvery soul car, surrounded by the other Seekers. Slowly the Seekers got inside their vehicles and drove off, leaving the main Seeker surveying the landscape. Key grip Bubba Sheffield

"On this production, even the soundstage was arduous, because we had dust and sand blowing around in there. I've had sand in my script book for months!"

—Sam Sullivan

stood outside the camera frame, holding a bounce card to help with the light. There was a cut, and Sheffield walked over to the line of production trucks.

"The terrain has been very challenging in some of the areas we've been shooting," he noted. "We were shooting on the cliff yesterday, and we had to try to keep our cameras steady. Our cameras and the mounts we have are gyro-stabilized, so that helps us quite a bit. Without those we wouldn't be able to get the shots over here and on top of the cliff and everything, because the wind would have just destroyed the shot. There's been so much shake and so much vibration nothing would have worked and we'd have actually had to call it a day."

Seekers scan the horizon searching for Wanderer, the rogue soul.

Shooting a desert scene with Kruger as the Seeker

In between shots, Andrew Niccol walked over to talk to the actors. The props department brought in a fabricated cattle carcass to add an unforgiving touch to the desert. One of the cameras telescoped out—it was the smaller kin to the seventy-three-inch Hydrascope that shot the wheat-field scenes in Baton Rouge. "This is the thirty-two-incher," Sheffield pointed out. "And you can get a shot from the air and see all the mesas and arroyos out here. The control itself—we call it the pickle—it's the scope in and out, and it's man-powered and has the gyro [stabilizer]. This is gorgeous, it really is. This crane is a beautiful piece of machinery."

Gaffer Paul Olinde

Although Friday would not be the last day, some of the cast and crew were moving on. Lee Hardee had wrapped his work as Aaron and was heading back to Louisiana—and, hopefully, another break at his next audition. The Seeker extras would be driven back to Albuquerque to catch their homeward flights.

The production ended up with fifteen official shooting days in New Mexico, one day over what was scheduled in the state and for the entire fifty-day shoot. Ray Angelic acknowledged the danger, as on any production, that things could have spun out of control into lost days and budget overruns. "It happens all the time. Generally, it's the job of a guy like myself to make sure you stay on budget and schedule. On this movie, we also had a responsible director in Andrew, and proactive producers in Stephenie, Nick, and Chockstone. If there was a budget concern, they worked it out with me by either reconceiving something or dropping it from the script. It's also a credit to our cast and crew, who all did their jobs well."

As principal photography had basically come in on time and budget, a bonus day was allowed to shoot a montage the DP called "all the new souls." After a travel day to Albuquerque, that Monday a small crew

"Every day has been a day I just chomped at the bit to get to work, to be here, because the lack of ostentation, the lack of egocentricity on the set, the simplicity of spirit, in the middle of a really complex film, has been just a delight for me. My last day, I don't want it to be my last day."

—William Hurt

worked on a greenscreen stage and exteriors to show a Masai warrior on the African plain, an Indian parent and child in a market, and a Parisian woman—their eyes all with the soul ring. "The around-the-world montage, showing how the souls have populated our entire planet, was something Andrew came up with in preproduction," Angelic said. "It was one of those things we hadn't budgeted, but it was important to Andrew. We kept it at the top of the wish list, and it was something we would do, provided the movie came in on time and on budget, or close to it."

"It was a nice slowdown at the end, because we got finished by five thirty, which was a short day and unusual for us," Roberto Schaefer said of the bonus day.

There had been enormous logistics in setting up the production, and it was a huge operation to close the show. The props department, which had taken to Shiprock guns, backpacks, an ax, a machete, a tire iron, a baseball bat, a soul Truth spray canister, binoculars, supplies from the Megamart, and a cow skeleton, packed everything up in a fifty-foot trailer and was on the road back to Los Angeles. "At the end of filming, we have another layer, which is our wrap," Guillaume Delouche explained. "It's very detailed, because you have to keep track of everything over the course of five or six months, including all the money you spent. Now it's about gathering up everything we made, purchased, or rented. We return all the rentals, inventory them, and make sure they're held until the movie is released, just in case we have to reshoot something. All the stuff that is the property of the production company has to be inventoried, photographed, and assessed to make sure it matches the money we spent, and then it's all shipped back to the production company with the manifest for the purposes of reshooting [if needed]. Once the movie comes

Niccol, Abel, and Ronan on location

out, these objects become part of American cinema lore, so you also have to make sure you know exactly where everything is."

After filming wrapped, all camera gear and equipment had to be taken to repair stations in Los Angeles for cleaning and fixing from sand and dust damage and infiltration. "The shoot was extremely challenging," Roberto Schaefer summed up shortly after principal photography was completed. "I always felt like we were kind of pushed, but I think most people had a good time. I enjoyed working with Andrew—even under stress, he kept things light. It all comes from the top."

In postproduction the film would come together in editing, along with the visual effects shots and musical score. From the DP's

Irons on set

side there was also the color-balancing phase to make sure each scene, which may have been shot in segments days, weeks, or months apart, looked as if it had been shot the same day and time and in the same weather conditions. The DI, or "digital intermediate," phase of editing allows filmmakers to make dramatic or subtle lighting and color changes that can alter the mood and look not only of a scene but of an entire movie. "I'll work with Ellen Somers to make sure the [background] plates fall into the right color space," Schaefer said of the visual effects shots. "We'll also use the DI to smooth things out and look consistent, because we went through a lot of different weather changes in scenes. With these digital things you can make blue red; green can become yellow. We'll also make the cave

William Hurt as Jeb, Scott Lawrence as Doc, Max Irons as Jared, Saoirse Ronan as Wanda, Chandler Canterbury as Jamie, and Jake Abel as Ian

world darker, dingy, and more realistic. We'll heighten the soul world to make it more shiny and chromelike.

"One day while we were shooting, I asked Andrew, 'Is the reason you wanted to shoot with the Alexa because you have these nice HD monitors and you can see everything cleanly, while on film you don't really see because you have standard-definition monitors and a video tap on the camera which is not accurate to the true image except for the framing?' And he goes, 'Yeah!' I told him Arri has film cameras now that have HD video taps that give you basically the same-quality video image. And he said, 'I could shoot on film again.' I realized the main reason he wanted to shoot digital was because of the quality of the image he could see on set. But it's all changing so fast—*three* new digital cameras came out in the time from when we started prep in late December to when we finished shooting."

After the Albuquerque portion of the New Mexico shoot, Nick Wechsler had left for Prague and other points in Europe; another movie was in the works for the producer. With *The Host* heading into postproduction, it was a good feeling to have crossed the finish line, all the challenges behind them. "The two most important things in getting this movie done were picking the right filmmaker in Andrew Niccol and picking Saoirse Ronan.

"For me, *The Host* is a much more serious and a deeper story than the Twilight novels. Those were just about romantic love—the way you feel about it when you're seventeen or eighteen, when there's nothing else in the world and you would do anything and be anything for love. That's a fun place to visit as a fantasy and it's fun to write. But *The Host* is more about the balance in life. It's not all about what you want romantically: there are so many other things that factor in and there are so many loves that can be stronger than that. And it just felt like a lot more grown up story."

—Stephenie Meyer

Abel and Ronan on set (left). Ronan with Irons on location (right).

Having good timing in the marketplace and being able to put together the money were also very attractive to Stephenie. That gave us the ultimate creative control. Nobody else would tell us what this film needed to be. We acted as a team, a family of filmmakers trying to achieve a collective vision."

The wrap-up was coming full circle for Meyer. She had finished writing *The Host* in 2006, before the cycle of Twilight Saga movies began. The irony was that the film adaptations of her novels had kept her from completing another. There had also been her Fickle Fish Films, whose first production would be *Austenland*, an adaptation of the novel by Shannon Hale.

"Since *Twilight* started four years ago, our world has really revolved around these films," said Meghan Hibbett. "I became Stephenie's assistant when the first Twilight movie was coming out, so together we kind of got tossed into the fire of this movie world."

"When I'm making a movie, there isn't the quiet and concentration time and lack of interruptions I need to write," Meyer reflected. "It's funny—my husband is an accountant, a math-oriented person, and for him the numbers always add up the same. Whether

There had been enormous logistics in setting up the production, and it was a huge operation to close the show.

he stops in the middle or comes back two days later, he's going to get the same answer. And it's just not like that with writing. I've had times when I've had half a chapter with everything working, but I left it for a bit and the thread of the idea was broken and I had to scrap the whole thing. You lose so much when you're interrupted. It's heartbreaking. The funny thing about movies is, you keep getting sucked in. It's a different kind of creativity, like using a different set of muscles."

The long hours, the pressure of getting the day's schedule, the battle against the elements—somehow it was all worth it. Everyone, from star to stuntman, from director to riggers, was in his or her own way living the dream. And something of each of them, invisible though it might be, would be up there on the screen.

"I'm very proud of this," Mustafa Harris said. "This is the first role I've ever had that I've been able to sink my teeth into. You never forget your first, and this is my first. I'm very grateful and proud to be part of it. It has a special place in my heart."

"This movie has been an amazing experience for me, my first from start to finish, from budget to com-

Hurt and Ronan perform a scene (left) and joke around on set (right).

pletion," Sam Hargrave concluded. "I've learned from Andrew, learned the business side from Ray [Angelic]. I learned as a stuntman, because I brought in the best and learned from them. For every aspect of this film, I learned something."

"When you're working on a movie, you want the story to be good, you want the people around you to be talented and passionate about their craft," Paul Olinde reflected. "It can be action, drama, horror, as long as the story is good and people are putting their heart and soul into it. For me, the lighting field is something I kind of got into by accident. As I mentioned earlier, you light a movie and hope not to be noticed. It's fun to be integral to the way a movie looks. You learn to love light."

For Saoirse Ronan, *The Host* was the latest stop in a promising career. She seemed to take it all—the critical recognition, an Academy Award nomination, the "Meryl Streep of her generation" accolades—with

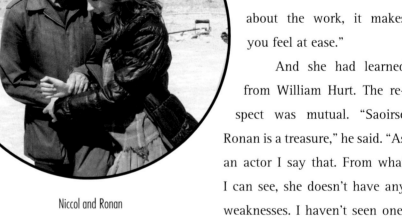

Niccol and Ronan

good grace and humor. On the production she learned a lot, starting with the director. "I met Andrew a while ago, and when I heard he was a Kiwi I loved him straightaway, because I love the Kiwis. He has a great sense of humor, and really cares about what he does. He doesn't think about anything but the film—he doesn't stop working. When you have someone who in a way is your leader, and he's so relaxed but still cares about the work, it makes you feel at ease."

And she had learned from William Hurt. The respect was mutual. "Saoirse Ronan is a treasure," he said. "As an actor I say that. From what I can see, she doesn't have any weaknesses. I haven't seen one. Never seen anything like it."

"It's been great having people like William," Ronan reflected. "One of my favorite scenes with William was a very simple drama scene, just the two of us sitting on a rock in Wanda's chamber, and he comes to apologize and say the humans will change their ways. Just the way the scene was written, and the mood we were both in, it just felt really great to do. William talks quite a bit about acting. I listen, because he knows more than I do and he's a true actor. He doesn't want to be a movie star. He just wants to be an actor and work with other actors. He feels it's very important to be part of an ensemble. He's the most experienced of all of us, and he's come in here and taken care of us and helped us. I've had a really great time with him, and we all worked well together.

"I can never really pinpoint what I learned on a film because the entire experience helps shape you, not only as an actor but as a person. I feel when I come off a film that I've grown up that little bit more, or learned a bit more, become a bit more experienced—just *lived* a bit more, you know?

"I remember Andrew said to me at the start, 'We're lucky to be in this line of work, because it's just fun. It should only ever be fun.'"

Irons, Ronan, and Canterbury

"There are a lot of dark arts to acting, a lot of technicality. At the same time, they call a play a play for a reason—because you're playing. What actors all have in common is we never let go of that ability to just play. That's the heart of it, I'd say."

—Max Irons

What was it that made this human love so much more desirable to me than the love of my own kind? Was it because it was exclusive and capricious? The souls offered love and acceptance to all. Did I crave a greater challenge? This love was tricky; it had no hard-and-fast rules — it might be given for free, as with Jamie, or earned through time and hard work, as with Ian, or completely and heartbreakingly unattainable, as with Jared.

Or was it simply better somehow? Because these humans could hate with so much fury, was the other end of the spectrum that they could love with more heart and zeal and fire?

I didn't know why I had yearned after it so desperately. All I knew was that, now that I had it, it was worth every ounce of risk and agony it had cost. It was better than I'd imagined.

It was everything.

Notes

1. Stephenie Meyer, *The Host* (New York: Little, Brown, trade paperback edition, 2010), pp. 90–91.

2. Mark A. Vieira, *Hollywood Horror: From Gothic to Cosmic* (New York: Abrams, 2003), pp. 156–57.

3. Meyer, *The Host*, p. 65.

4. Andy Nicholson produced his notes for the production in May 2012 and made them available for this book.

5. Meyer, *The Host*, p. 47.

6. Ibid., p. 6.

7. Ibid., p. 484.

8. Ibid., p. 472.

Acknowledgments

I'm grateful to editor Asya Muchnick for her support and stellar work on this book (Asya also edited Stephenie Meyer's *The Host*). And a bow and a tip of the hat to editor Erin Stein, who recommended me for this project and did such a terrific job on the Twilight Saga movie companion books.

I'm grateful to the entire production team of *The Host*, who went above and beyond in their support for this book. I'm particularly thankful to Nick Wechsler and Ray Angelic, Lizzy Bradford and Felicity Aldridge at Nick Wechsler Productions, and Matt McKinney, assistant to Andrew Niccol. I'll always be grateful to the amazing unit publicist Louise Spencer, who was superb in arranging interviews during my visit to Shiprock (and got us both out ahead of the sandstorm that shut down the show). My thanks as well to Sara Lou Hartman and the rest of the good folks who kept everything running smoothly at base camp, and to production coordinator Janie Elliott for all the courtesies in Farmington. And here's a toast to unit stills photographer Alan Markfield, a former globe-trotting photojournalist and storied picture-taker whose work graces this book. Thanks also to the studio for making available Electronic Press Kit transcripts, from which select quotes were taken.

My thanks to my agent, John Silbersack, for his dedication and continuing efforts on my behalf, and to his intrepid assistant, Rachel Mosner. Love to my dear Edris for her patience and support, and to my mother, Bettylu, who did her usual great job of proofreading my manuscript, and a high five to my nephew and computer wizard, Michael Vaz, for a little high-tech help.

And to Mike Wigner, World's Greatest Bike Messenger: Wig, it's a wrap—see you at Vesuvio's!

Rose Ann Habershaw

About the Author

Mark Cotta Vaz is the author of the number one *New York Times* bestselling Twilight Saga movie companion series. He is also the author of thirty-two books, including *Industrial Light + Magic: Into the Digital Realm*, a history of the second decade of George Lucas's famed visual effects house; the award-winning *The Invisible Art: The Legends of Movie Matte Painting* (coauthored with Academy governor and Oscar winner Craig Barron); and the critically acclaimed *Living Dangerously:*